THE OFFICIAL  SPORT
EURO 04
FACT FILE

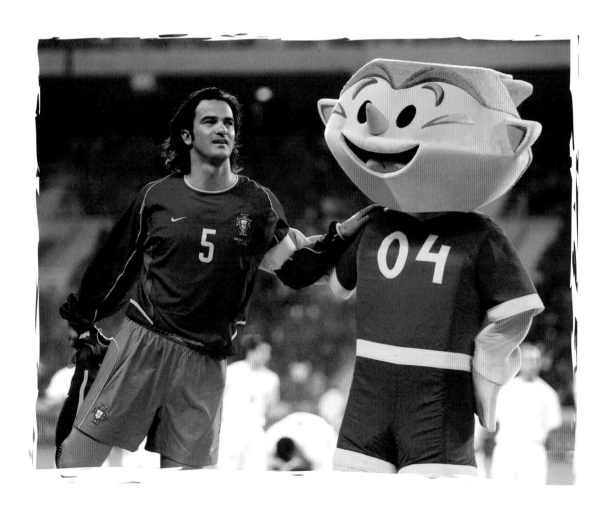

THE OFFICIAL itv SPORT
EURO 04
FACT FILE

First published by Carlton Books 2004

Copyright © Carlton Books Limited 2004

A CIP catalogue record for this book is available upon request.

ISBN 1 84442 862 1

Project Editor: Nigel Matheson
Project Art Direction: Darren Jordan
Picture Research: Stephen O'Kelly
Production: Lisa French

Carlton Books Ltd
20 Mortimer Street
London W1T 3JW

Printed and bound in Portugal

CARLTON BOOKS

Right: Spot-kick king: David Beckham turns away in triumph after scoring the winning goal from a penalty against Macedonia in Skopje. The final score was 2–1 **Previous page:** Super-sub: Portugal defender Fernando Couto warms up with Kinas, the mascot for this year's championships, before a friendly with Greece

CONTENTS

Right: *Allez les Bleus:* the French squad celebrate after David Trezeguet's golden goal gave them the European crown to set alongside the mantle of world champions from 1998. France beat Italy 2–1 aet in the 2000 final in Rotterdam

INTRODUCTION

Europe's football federation celebrates its 50th birthday this year. What better way to bring UEFA's festivities to a grand climax than by staging the most outstanding finals in the history of the European Championship? This year's tournament has everything going for it, from great stadia to a roll call of superstars, and the prospect of seeing Europe's top 16 nations go head to head in the Portuguese sun is truly mouthwatering for fans of the beautiful game.

No expense or effort is being spared for the jubilee party by both European football officials and their counterparts in Portuguese sport and politics. The hosts want their soccer spectacular in the summer sun to be the hottest in the history of the event – not because of the soaring temperatures which pose their own challenge for the players – but because of the passion and intensity of the football.

These are, after all, the 16 current top nations in Europe and the stage is a sparkling 10-strong package of stadia, including redeveloped and rebuilt 'legends' such as Benfica's Estadio da Luz which hosts the final on July 4. The roll call of stars reads like a football *Who's Who*. The biggest stars from the greatest clubs will turn fans' loyalties inside out as they leave the club world behind and pull on their national colours.

Real Madrid, from neighbouring Spain, set the standard. Injuries permitting, Portugal's Luis Figo will cross first-round swords with team-mate Raul of Spain in Group A, while Group B sees England's David Beckham duelling for control of midfield with France's World Player of the Year Zinedine Zidane.

Eight past champions, bearing in mind intervening political changes, will be competing: the Czech Republic, Denmark, France, Germany, Holland, Italy, Russia and Spain. Three of those – France, Germany and Italy – are also former World Cup winners.

The qualifying competition was packed with drama right down to the closing minutes of the play-offs when newcomers Latvia sprang a major shock by knocking out Turkey. That maintained the jinx on nations who finish third in the previous World Cup. Poland, third in the World Cups in 1974 and 1982, failed to make it to the 1976 and 1984 European finals; the same fate befell France (third in Mexico in 1986), Italy (third as hosts in 1990), Sweden (third in the US in 1994) and Croatia (third in France in 1998).

But other nations went on rewriting the European record books. Six nations reached the 100-match milestone in the qualifiers – the Czech Republic, Denmark, France, Holland, Russia and Spain. Four of those nations – France, Holland, Russia and Spain – also topped 200 goals in

Right: The balloons go up: the opening ceremony of the European Championship in 2000 at the King Baudoin Stadium in Brussels, formerly the Heysel Stadium

the competition. On a notional basis of three points for a win, Spain head the all-time achievement list with 208 points from 106 matches in qualifying and finals, one point ahead of both Russia and Holland.

Lennart Johansson, UEFA's long-serving Swedish president, says: "I've been around quite a while now and I've seen many tournament preparations. This one is not only as well-prepared as the others, it's even better because of the enthusiasm of everyone involved in the local organization on the ground in Portugal."

Not that it has always been that way. Only 17 nations entered the inaugural championship in 1958–60 when disdainful Italy, West Germany and England were among the absentees. It was no great money-maker for UEFA either, and they depended on the generosity of the French federation to supply a trophy based on a design from the artefacts of Ancient Greece.

Of course, since then, tournament finances have been revolutionised beyond description by the advent of sponsorship and television.

UEFA will hand out a total of £80m in prize and participation cash to the finalists which is half as much again as their share four years ago after the first co-hosted event in Belgium and Holland.

The cash will be paid from the estimated £550m which UEFA expects to generate from television, sponsorship, ticketing and tournament hospitality. A further cache of £170m will be shared among all UEFA's 52 member associations and other sums will be allocated to support youth and women's football, refereeing, coaching and allied development projects.

Each of the 16 finalists will be paid £3.2m for turning up, and the winners of each group match will receive £420,000 with £210,000 for the draw. Any nation who win all their first-round matches will thus be guaranteed £1.2m – that and a place in the quarter-finals!

The eight quarter-finalists will receive a further £1.2m each, the semi-finalists £1.8m each, the runners-up a further £2.5m and the winners £4.3m. But, of course, what will matter more than the money will be the glory and the guaranteed place in football history. For fans the world over, that is what Euro 2004 is really all about.

Final Tournament Attendances

Year		Teams	Played	Total	Average
1960	France	4	4	78,958	19,838
1964	Spain	4	4	156,253	39,063
1968	Italy	4	5	260,939	52,187
1972	Belgium	4	4	106,510	26,627
1976	Yugoslavia	4	4	106,087	26,522
1980	Italy	8	14	350,665	25,048
1984	France	8	15	599,655	39,977
1988	Germany	8	15	849,844	56,656
1992	Sweden	8	15	429,241	28,616
1996	England	16	31	1,276,171	41,167
2000	Belgium /Holland	16	31	1,126,443	36,337
Total		–	142	5,340,756	37,612

THE DRAW

The entertainment which wrapped up the draw in the Atlantico Pavilion at the Lisbon Expo complex climaxed with a spectacular drumming display from the Toca Rufar folk group. Their drum roll was an appropriate prelude for the thundering football to come. In the opening rounds, Spain play Portugal and France meet England, while newcomers Latvia prepare for a baptism of fire in the 'Group of Death' featuring the Czech Republic, Germany and Holland.

Gerhard Aigner was thrilled with the outcome of the draw which he presided over for the last time before his retirement as chief executive of UEFA, the European federation.

Group A matched hosts Portugal with their eastern neighbours Spain; holders France would start their defence in Group B against England; Nordic neighbours Denmark and Sweden were drawn with Italy in Group C; newcomers Latvia found themselves in the so-called 'Group of Death' with three previous winners in the Czech Republic, Germany and Holland.

Hosts Portugal kick off the extravaganza when they face Greece on June 12 in the new Dragao stadium in Oporto. The nations have faced each other competitively on only two previous occasions, in the European qualifiers in 1991, with each winning their home tie. But the most important match for the Portuguese will be their duel with neighbours Spain on June 20 in the Alvalade stadium, home of Sporting Lisbon.

Pride will be doubly at stake since Portugal beat Spain decisively in the race to win hosting rights to the finals. Then again, Spain will also have one eye on their game with Greece who surprisingly pipped Raul and Co to top spot in their qualifying group.

Group B gets under way with its most eagerly awaited match when France face England in Benfica's new Luz stadium. But it will certainly not be the nations' first meeting in a finals tournament. England defeated France 2–0 on their way to winning the World Cup in 1966 and beat them 3–1 in the nations' opening match at the 1982 World Cup in Spain – when Bryan Robson struck the opening goal after only 27 seconds.

In the European finals, the teams shared an off-key goalless draw in Sweden in 1992. England will face more old foes in Switzerland with whom they drew 1–1 at Wembley in the opening match of Euro 96 when Alan Shearer and Kubilay Turkilmaz scored the goals. France have even more recent memories of Croatia – having hit back from a goal down to beat them 2–1 in the semi-finals of the 1998 World Cup. Defender Lilian Thuram struck both French goals.

UEFA had seeded the 16 finalists in advance to try to ensure a balanced competition. Yet Group C still managed to match four teams who had all won their qualifying groups. Italy, runners-up four years ago on a golden goal in Rotterdam, open up with an awkward test against Denmark in Guimaraes but Sweden were delighted with the omens that see them launch against Bulgaria.

The Swedes defeated the Bulgarians home and away in the Euro 2000 qualifiers and, further back, thrashed them 5–0 in the third place play-off at the 1994 World Cup.

Latvia were always going to face an uphill task but the draw placed them in a Group D which could hardly have appeared any more intimidating for the newcomers from the Baltic. Far more experienced international outfits would have quailed at the prospects of duelling with three former winners in Germany, Holland and the Czech Republic.

Latvia begin against the Czechs, while Holland and Germany are renewing their long-time rivalry. The most memorable meeting was the 1974 World Cup Final when the West German hosts conceded a second-minute penalty but recovered to win 2–1. The nations then met three times subsequently in the European finals, with the balance currently standing 2–1 in favour of Holland.

Germany won 3–2 in a first-round group match in Naples in 1980, while Holland won the 1988 semi-final 2–1 and a group match 3–1 in 1992. German coach Rudi Voller knows all about the tensions and complexities of the duel, both tactically and psychologically, after having played in the latter two matches. He was also sent off when the Germans beat Holland 2–1 in a World Cup second-round tie in 1990.

The Czechs bring an added complication to the equation, recalling memories of the 1976 finals when Czechoslovakia beat Holland 3–1 after extra-time in the semi-final and West Germany on penalties in the final. The Germans had to wait until 1996 for revenge by defeating the Czechs 2–1 on a golden goal in the final.

Of course, the Czechs' clash with Holland is another reprise from the qualifying competition where Karek Bruckner's men pipped the Dutch for top spot in the group. "We've beaten them before – and the Germans," said Bruckner. "You always have to think positive and I am sure that's what all 16 of us will all be doing."

Right: *Luck of the draw: UEFA CEO Gerhard Aigner supervises proceedings at the Atlantico Pavilion as the names come out of the hat to determine who plays who*

THE VENUES

Portugal's hosting of Euro 2004 is a triumph for the powers of Portuguese persuasion as well as football tradition. It is also a reward for a massive investment in infrastructure which will see the 31 matches staged in a batch of the newest stadia anywhere in Europe. Small is beautiful is the idea behind these finals and, from Porto in the North to Faro in the South, everything is in place for a tournament which promises to give football its soul back.

ritish sailors and engineers brought football to Portugal in the early 1860s and Euro 2004 will be the biggest of the sports events the country has seen in all those 140 succeeding years.

To make the most of the festival, the national and local authorities have arranged to finance five new stadia and redeveloped an equal number so comprehensively that they will be as good as new when the finals kick off on June 12 in Oporto.

Yet when Portugal stated its intention to bid to host Euro 2004, the rest of European football laughed. It appeared to be an impossible challenge in the face of competition from mighty neighbours Spain and the intriguing central European partnership of Austria and Hungary.

When the executive committee of UEFA, the European federation, came to vote in the autumn of 1999 the joke was on the traditionalists. Complacent Spain gathered a humiliating handful of votes; the so-called 'Danube option' of Austro-Hungary took no votes at all. Portugal completely swept the board.

That result was a massive achievement for the federation, for the government and also for Carlos Cruz, the television chat-show host turned bid director. But Cruz's arguments struck a popular chord beyond the game's politicians.

He had campaigned bravely and aggressively, in an increasingly centralised and commercial sporting world, for the international game to "give the finals to Portugal for the sake of football's soul".

Cruz argued that hosting the big events should not be the exclusive preserve of the neighbouring football giants of western Europe. He had identified an issue on which even the club presidents of deadly rivals Benfica, Sporting and FC Porto could unite.

Portugal's successful hosting of Expo 98 had provided an injection of national self-confidence, underpinned by European community investment made clear in the development of the country's airports and highways.

Cruz claimed: "We can organise the finals in an almost perfect way. We are building five new stadia with financial support from the government and redeveloping five other stadia so thoroughly that they will, in effect, be new stadia. We have had great players and great teams down the years. We cannot let that momentum go to waste.

"Also, we are a safe country with no problems politically or socially. We have new roads. Good hotels. We are such a small country that you can go from north to south in two hours. So the teams can rest, recuperate, train and prepare properly. They don't need to be always travelling. That's got to be good for the standard of football."

Winning the vote within UEFA was the signal Portugal needed for the government to go ahead with an ambitious national sports facilities project. The new stadia and the other sports facilities incorporated in the various developments will serve the country well for years to come.

The stadia have not been built to the 40,000-capacity minimum models seen at the 2002 World Cup finals in South Korea and Japan. But UEFA does not demand such extravagance. The European Championship lasts but a month – the domestic game must support and maintain the stadia for years after the circus has left town.

UEFA's minimum demand is that a European Championship host nation has at least one stadium of 50,000, one of 40,000 and the remainder of at least 30,000. By that rating, Portugal fits the bill with a little to spare; it has actually given UEFA more than it asked. Seven of the stadia boast 30,000 capacities, two stretch to 52,000, with the largest being the new home of Benfica at 65,000.

Football was brought to Portugal by British expats in Lisbon in the early 1860s and was played informally by Britons only for the next decade or so. The Lisbon Football Club was formed in 1875 and the first formally reported game had to wait until 1888 in nearby Cascais.

Portuguese students returning from England in the 1890s brought a passion for the game back with them and rapidly took over the local scene. FC Porto was founded in 1893, Benfica in 1904, Sporting in 1906 and the Portuguese federation in 1914. A national team was launched in 1921, and Portugal first entered the World Cup in 1934.

Not until Portuguese clubs began raiding the African colonies of Angola and Mozambique in the 1950s did the country's football come alive. Benfica benefited the most. They won the European Cup in 1961 and 1962 – and were runners-up three more times in the next six years – thanks to African impetus. Angolan-born stars such as goalkeeper Alberto Costa Pereira and centre-forward Jose Aguas were complemented by

Mozambique discoveries such as playmaker Mario Coluna and, of course, the incomparable Eusebio.

In 1966 Portugal achieved their best-ever World Cup finish of third in England. In the first round they beat Hungary, Brazil and Bulgaria and then hit back from 3–0 down to defeat North Korea 5–3 in an amazing quarter-final. Next time out Portugal lost 2–1 to their English hosts in the semi-finals but they returned to Wembley two days later to beat the Soviet Union by the same margin in the third-place play-off. Eusebio and Jose Torres scored the goals for a Portuguese side made up of five players from Benfica, three from Sporting and one apiece from Porto, Belenenses and Vitoria Setubal.

Overall, however, it remains the clubs who have brought home the international prizes at senior level. Benfica boast their European Cup double plus five further appearances in the final; neighbours Sporting won the Cup-winners Cup in 1964; and FC Porto carried off the treble of World Club Cup, European Cup and European Supercup in 1987 then added the UEFA Cup in 2003.

The story at junior level has been different, however. Portugal are one of the most successful producers of youth talent in Europe if not the world. In both 1989 and 1991 they won the World Youth Cup and the legacy, in terms of players such as Luis Figo, Joao Pinto and Manuel Rui Costa, took Portugal to the semi-finals of the last European Championship in 2000.

The so-called 'golden generation' came within a golden goal of a place in the final. They believe home advantage should make the difference – especially given the passionate support generated in their superb new homes.

THE STADIA

Aveiro

Stadium: Municipal
Capacity: 30,000
Hosting: two group matches
Club: Beira-Mar

This new stadium is in the City Sports Park, a project which also features a multi-purpose indoor arena, golf course, leisure park, swimming pools and six hotels. The stadium, three miles from the town centre, is the new home of local side SC Beira-Mar whose old 14,000-capacity Mario Duarte stadium could not be redeveloped to meet UEFA's exacting European Championship standards.

Braga

Stadium: Municipal
Capacity: 30,000
Hosting: two group matches
Club: Sporting Braga

The spectacular new Braga stadium was described as a "work of art" by UEFA's stadium security supremo, Ernie Walker. It has been built on the Monte Castro hills, one the city's highest points. The local railway station is two miles away and a motorway link has been incorporated into the Parque Urban complex which also features a 2,000-seater multi-purpose indoor arena, an Olympic-size swimming pool, football training pitches and tennis courts.

Coimbra

Stadium: Municipal
Capacity: 30,000
Hosting: two group matches
Club: Academica de Coimbra

The existing stadium has been redeveloped to double the original 15,000-capacity even though one end of the U-shape will be cut away and the athletics track has been retained. The surrounding land includes a multi-purpose sports hall, Olympic-size pool, multiplex cinema, underground car park, plus commercial and office developments.

Faro

Stadium: Algarve
Capacity: 30,000
Hosting: two group matches and one quarter-final
Club: SC Farense

The new Estadio Algarve has been built in the Cities' Park midway between Faro and Loule in Portugal's most popular tourist region. The design allows for further development after the finals to incorporate an athletics track. The surrounds include two training pitches, a heliport, botanical garden, lake and nine-hole golf course as well as a separate mini-stadium for athletics.

Guimaraes

Stadium: Afonso Henriques
Capacity: 30,000
Hosting: two group matches
Club: Vitoria Guimaraes

This redeveloped stadium is in the city centre, only a few minutes by foot from Praca do Toural, the most popular square. Lifts as well as new stairways have been incorporated into the Vitoria club's new home. The stadium takes its name from its medieval status as birthplace of Afonso Henriques, first king of Portugal.

Leiria

Stadium: Magalhães Pessoa
Capacity: 30,000
Hosting: two group matches
Club: Uniao Leiria

Three new stands and roofing have been built to raise capacity to the necessary minimum 30,000 from its original 11,000. The stadium, key feature of the Leiria sports complex, is owned and administered by the local council.

Lisbon

Stadium: Jose Alvalade
Capacity: 52,000
Hosting: three group matches, one quarter-final and one semi-final
Club: Sporting Clube de Portugal

Sporting Clube's new home has been built on land adjacent to the original stadium and named in honour of one of their original patrons, the Viscount of Alvalade. The new stadium is as notable a landmark for arriving air travellers as was the old one with its seating tiers in Sporting's traditional green and white. A wide variety of other sports facilities as well as apartments, shops, a medical centre, restaurants, bars, multiplex cinema and bowling alley have been incorporated. The stadium is served by Lisbon's underground system.

Lisbon

Stadium: Luz
Capacity: 65,000
Hosting: three group matches, one quarter-final and the final
Club: Benfica

Benfica's new home is still the biggest stadium in Lisbon. Modern security and fan comfort demands, however, mean it is little more than half the size of the old Estadio da Luz which welcomed 120,000 for the 1991 World Youth Cup final. Portugal beat Brazil on penalties in that historic clash after a goalless draw. The stadium's other major international occasion was the 1992 European Cup-winners' Cup Final in which Werder Bremen beat Monaco 2–0. Appropriately, Benfica will be hosting the Euro 2004 Final in the club's centenary year and 50 years after the original Luz stadium was opened. Architect Damon Lavelle's development includes the club's famous museum, a health club, family restaurants, conference halls and an entertainment centre, plus first-rate facilities for basketball, roller hockey, volleyball, five-a-side football, billiards and badminton.

Porto

Stadium: Dragao
Capacity: 52,000
Hosting: opening match and two other group matches, one quarter-final and one semi-final
Club: FC Porto

The new 'Dragons' stadium, with a translucent roof, is next door to the old Estadio das Antas. Thus it forms the centre-piece of the region's projected 'sports city'. The surrounding area has been completely transformed with a commercial centre, residential areas and a multi-purpose indoor arena.

Porto

Stadium: Bessa
Capacity: 30,000
Hosting: three group matches
Club: Boavista

Boavista's traditional home has been virtually rebuilt with four new full-covered stands in what the architects have described as "the English football style". Further sports facilities are planned for the surrounding complex which is well served by local transport facilities including a heliport.

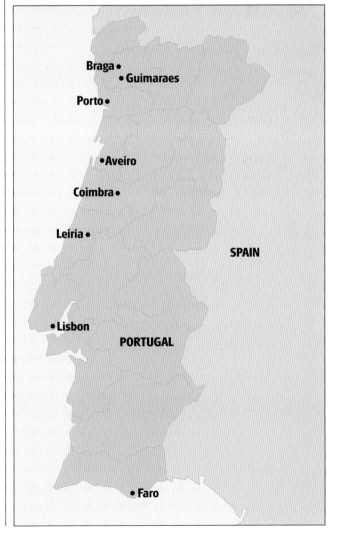

FIXTURES

The draw has thrown up more than its fair share of exciting clashes between old rivals. At a team level, Spain v Portugal should provide a fitting climax to Group A, while France v England, Denmark v Sweden and Germany v Holland look to be the pick of the other groups. As for individual players, the first round brings David Beckham versus Thierry Henry, Raul against Figo and Michael Ballack into conflict with Edgar Davids. What more could you ask for?

ompared to the last World Cup in Korea and Japan where there were vast distances, even oceans, between the different venues, this year's tournament is a model of compactness. Journey times allow group games to be split between different regions of Portugal, allowing the host nation to play in the capital Lisbon as well as Porto in the North. **(Please see page 79 for the later rounds.)**

GROUP A

| Portugal | Greece | Spain | Russia |

Match 1: Saturday June 12   5.00pm
PORTUGAL v GREECE
Dragao, Porto

Match 2: Saturday June 12   7.45pm
SPAIN v RUSSIA
Algarve, Faro/Loule

Match 9: Wednesday June 16   5.00pm
GREECE v SPAIN
Bessa, Porto

Match 10: Wednesday June 16   7.45pm
RUSSIA v PORTUGAL
Luz, Lisbon

Match 17: Sunday June 20   7.45pm
RUSSIA v GREECE
Algarve, Faro/Loule

Match 18: Sunday June 20   7.45pm
SPAIN v PORTUGAL
Jose Alvalade, Lisbon

GROUP B

| France | England | Switzerland | Croatia |

Match 3: Sunday June 13   5.00pm
SWITZERLAND v CROATIA
Estadio Municipal de Leiria

Match 4: Sunday June 13   7.45pm
FRANCE v ENGLAND
Luz, Lisbon

Match 11: Thursday June 17   5.00pm
ENGLAND v SWITZERLAND
Municipal, Coimbra

Match 12: Thursday June 17   7.45pm
CROATIA v FRANCE
Estadio Municipal de Leiria

Match 19: Monday June 21   7.45pm
CROATIA v ENGLAND
Luz, Lisbon

Match 20: Monday June 21   7.45pm
SWITZERLAND v FRANCE
Municipal, Coimbra

GROUP C

Bulgaria　　**Denmark**　　**Italy**　　**Sweden**

Match 5: Monday June 14   5.00pm
DENMARK v ITALY
Afonso Henriques, Guimaraes

Match 6: Monday June 14   7.45pm
SWEDEN v BULGARIA
Jose Alvalade, Lisbon

Match 13: Friday June 18   5.00pm
BULGARIA v DENMARK
Municipal, Braga

Match 14: Friday June 18   7.45pm
ITALY v SWEDEN
Dragao, Porto

Match 21: Tuesday June 22   7.45pm
DENMARK v SWEDEN
Bessa, Porto

Match 22: Tuesday June 22   7.45pm
ITALY v BULGARIA
Afonso Henriques, Guimaraes

GROUP D

Latvia　　**Holland**　　**Germany**　　**Czech Republic**

Match 7: Tuesday June 15   5.00pm
CZECH REPUBLIC v LATVIA
Municipal, Aveiro

Match 8: Tuesday June 15   7.45pm
GERMANY v HOLLAND
Dragao, Porto

Match 15: Saturday June 19   5.00pm
LATVIA v GERMANY
Bessa, Porto

Match 16: Saturday June 19   7.45pm
HOLLAND v CZECH REPUBLIC
Municipal, Aveiro

Match 23: Wednesday June 23 7.45pm
GERMANY v CZECH REPUBLIC
Jose Alvalade, Lisbon

Match 24: Wednesday June 23 7.45pm
HOLLAND v LATVIA
Municipal, Braga

Left: Beware of the Pit Bull: Torsten Frings and Marko Rehmer take on Edgar Davids during the friendly in Gelsenkirchen in 2002 when Holland beat Germany 3–1

HOW THEY QUALIFIED

Holders France led the way by winning all eight of their matches in group one. Zinedine Zidane and Co dispelled memories of their World Cup disaster by scoring 29 goals and conceding only two. Just like the Czech Republic, Sweden and Bulgaria, they secured their ticket for the finals with one round of matches remaining. Having put their dismal performances in Korea and Japan behind them, France look like hot favourites this summer.

*L*es Bleus collected the necessary point with a 2–0 win in Slovenia. Goals from David Trezeguet and Olivier Dacourt delighted coach Jacques Santini after "our toughest match in the group". Slovenia's consolation was to find they had finished runners-up since Israel had been held 2–2 by Malta at their home from home in Antalya, Turkey.

In Group Three, the Czechs' hero was their Euro 96 inspiration Karel Poborsky. The decisive game matched the Czechs against Holland. Poborsky was fouled for Jan Koller's penalty then scored the second on 38 minutes. Edgar Davids was sent off for the penalty-conceding foul. Rafael Van der Vaart pulled one back, so the Czechs had to wait to celebrate until Milan Baros struck in extra-time.

The players hoisted coach Karel Bruckner onto their shoulders after extending his personal unbeaten run to 17 matches. The Dutch had no excuse. Skipper Frank De Boer said: "We started poorly and our passing was terrible."

Sweden made a slow start in Group Four with draws against Latvia and Hungary but five wins in a row then lifted them into a top spot they never relinquished. Having qualified, the Swedes were surprisingly beaten 1–0 at home in their last game by Latvia. Maris Verpakovskis edged the Baltic nation into runners-up spot ahead of Poland.

Bulgaria's young team were underestimated by their group rivals, Belgium, who slumped 2–0 at home to Plamen Markov's men first time out. The Bulgars booked their place in Portugal with a 3–0 win in Andorra which qualified them with a game to spare. They lost their unbeaten record on the last matchday, however, against Croatia whose 1–0 win meant they pipped Belgium into runners-up spot on head-to-head record.

The contentious head-to-head rating also proved crucial in Group Two. The 1992 champions Denmark finished top with a draw in Bosnia-Herzegovina. Norway took runners-up spot ahead of Romania despite a goal difference of plus-four compared with the east Europeans' plus-12.

Group Five went Germany's way but it was far from plain sailing. Coach Rudi Voller let rip at media critics who included ex-international Gunter Netzer after a depressing goalless draw in Iceland.

Voller's fury – "I'm not nailed to the bench like Vogts and Ribbeck before me, I don't need all this nonsense" – delighted his players who responded with a 2–1 home win over Scotland. Goals from Fredi Bobic and Michael Ballack inflicted the first competitive defeat of Berti Vogts's reign over Scotland who had Maurice Ross sent off.

Ballack, Bobic and newcomer Kevin Kuranyi duly led the Germans to Portugal via a 3–0 home win over Iceland. Scotland grabbed the play-off slot after Darren Fletcher's lone goal beat Lithuania.

In Group Six, Greece came from behind to surprise Spain. The Greeks lost 2–0 at home to the Spaniards in the opening fixture but turned the group around after a Stelios Giannakopoulos goal brought them a shock 1–0 win back in Zaragoza.

Controversy erupted when Armenia accused the Greeks of trying to 'buy' their next away match in Yerevan. UEFA investigated, found no proof, and duly ratified the 1–0 win which fired the Greeks forward to win the group. Spain also won in Armenia, by 4–0 on the last matchday. But Greece stayed one point clear by virtue of the Vasilis Tsartas penalty which defeated Northern Ireland.

Group Seven turned on the renewal of hostilities between England and Turkey. Sven-Goran Eriksson's trump card was the Everton 17-year-old Wayne Rooney who became the youngest England marksman of all time in a 2–1 comeback win over Macedonia. He was on target again in the 2–0 follow-up win over Liechtenstein which saw David Beckham's return to Old Trafford after his Real Madrid move.

Liechtenstein's manager Walter Horrmann was not impressed, saying: "England will find it very hard getting the point they need in Istanbul." But he was wrong. Turkey lost their heads and with it their cohesion. Beckham missed a penalty but it did not matter. The Turks only showed their fighting spirit in the players' tunnel when a goalless draw confirmed England as group-winners.

Wales were quickest out of the blocks in Group Nine, winning 2–0 in Finland, 2–1 at home to Italy then both away and home against distant Azerbaijan. But their momentum was tragically lost after a politically enforced postponement of their visit to Serb capital Belgrade where the Welsh later lost 2–0. Italy twisted the group around by running Wales ragged in Milan. Pippo Inzaghi scored a hat-trick in the 4–0 win which inspired Italy to go top.

Group Ten was the tightest of all with only eight points separating Switzerland, Russia, the Republic of Ireland, Albania and Georgia. The Swiss were unbeaten for their first six games and beat Ireland 2–0 in Basel in their decisive tie to win the group. Russia came back from the brink to snatch runners-up spot. The Irish were third, three points further back. They missed the drive of Roy Keane and never recovered from a poor start which saw Mick McCarthy replaced as manager by Brian Kerr.

The play-offs brought 'lucky loser' success for Croatia, Holland, Russia and Spain but will be remembered for Latvia's humbling of Turkey.

Latvia won the first leg 1–0 in freezing Riga but in Istanbul Turkey seized a 2–0 lead after 64 minutes through goals from Ilhan Mansiz and veteran Hakan Sukur. Fatally, then, they relaxed. Two minutes later, Latvia pulled level overall when Juris Laizans's free-kick swirled deceptively beyond the goalkeeper Omer Catkic.

A silent crowd saw Turkey throw men forward and then witnessed Latvia exploit the gaps. Twelve minutes remained when a long ball over the top sent Verpakovskis clear to hold off Bulent Korkmaz and score number two. Turkey were out and Latvia, remarkably, were through.

Croatia relied on the Midas touch of Monaco striker Dado Prso to edge past their Balkan neighbours Slovenia. Prso came off a four-goal extravaganza against Deportivo in the Champions League to grab Croatia's goal in the opening 1–1 draw in Zagreb. He subsequently struck the lone winner in the return after the Croats had been reduced to 10 men by the expulsion of Igor Tudor.

Holland approached their duel with Scotland squabbling like schoolboys and were caned 1–0 at Hampden. But James McFadden's stylish goal proved inadequate when the Dutch handed out a 6–0 lesson back in Amsterdam to puncture the brief euphoria of the Tartan Army.

A second British disappointment saw Wales edged out by Russia. Manager Mark Hughes plotted an effective containment operation in Moscow. But it all went to waste when Vadim Yevseyev snatched the tie's only goal after a 22nd-minute break back in Cardiff.

Finally, Spain returned to the finals with surprising ease. They scrambled a 2–1 home win over Norway, courtesy of Raul and a late own goal from Henning Berg. But in Oslo Raul struck again on the half hour and Juan Carlos Valeron inspired second-half goals for Vicente and Joseba Etxeberria.

After 210 games, 438 days and 566 goals, the qualifying competition was history.

Above: Baltic triumph: Mihails Zemlinskis and captain Vitalijs Astafjevs of Latvia celebrate qualifying for the finals after their amazing 2–2 draw in Istanbul

GREAT MOMENTS FROM THE PAST

The first European Championship gets under way under the title of the Nations Cup and Lev Yashin's Soviet Union set the ball rolling to make history as the very first champions... Suarez and Amancio's Spain grab the glory in Madrid four years later to become the first winning hosts... then Italy struggle all the way but make it second time lucky in Rome after winning the only replayed final in championship history.

natoly Ilyin scored the historic first goal in the European Championship – then labelled the Nations Cup – on September 28, 1958, in a 3–1 win for the Soviet Union over Hungary. The Soviets duly powered on to the finals which, in honour of the event's founding father Henri Delaunay, were staged in France.

France staged the first finals. Four nations were involved, playing knock-out semi-finals, with a third-place play-off and final. France should have been in that final themselves. They led Yugoslavia 4–2 in their semi-final opener with 15 minutes to play.

The Slavs, however, were spurred on by a sense of injustice over the second of Francois Heutte's two goals which should have been disallowed for offside. They thus battled back with astonishing results – putting three goals past Georges Lamia in the France goal within three minutes. French fans excused the result on the grounds that playmaker Raymond Kopa and star striker Juste Fontaine were out injured. Lamia, his confidence shattered by the Slavs' great revival, never played for France again.

The Soviet Union, including legendary goalkeeper Lev Yashin, thrashed Czechoslovakia 3–0 in Marseille in the other semi-final. Valentin Ivanov scored twice.

The final was played in the old Parc des Princes – just like the first European Cup final four years earlier. The first goal was almost an own goal, Soviet skipper Igor Netto deflecting a strike from Milan Galic though the latter was credited with the goal just two minutes before the interval. Soviet right-wing Slava Metreveli equalised four minutes after half-time to

Above: Victory rites of 'The Black Octopus': goalkeeper Lev Yashin parades the first European Championship cup after victory over Yugoslavia in Paris **Right:** All roads lead to Rome for Italian goalkeeping legend Dino Zoff, who kept a clean sheet as Italy (in the dark shirts) beat Yugoslavia 2–0 in the replayed final of 1968

send the final into extra-time. Yugoslavia had been the better team. Only the brilliance of Lev Yashin in the Soviet goal had denied them victory. But in extra-time they lost heart and defensive discipline. Soviet centre-forward Viktor Ponedelnik snatched his one chance of the game and the Soviet Union were the first European champions.

The 1964 tournament saw England enter for the first time – only to crash out in the first round. Alf Ramsey's first competitive experience in charge ended in a 6–3 aggregate defeat by France. The finals were staged in Spain who put their faith in a new generation of home-grown youngsters. The final four were completed by the Soviet holders, Hungary and Denmark.

Yashin and Co beat Denmark easily, by 3–0, but Spain needed extra-time to defeat Hungary 2–1. Real Madrid's new hero Amancio scored the winner, five minutes from the end. Spain's most influential player was Luis Suarez from Inter Milan who pulled the midfield strings.

Spain took an early lead against the Soviets in the final in the Estadio Bernabeu through Jesus Pereda. Galinzjan Khusainov struck back for the Soviet Union, but a second-half strike from Zaragoza centre-forward Marcelino was the signal for Spanish celebrations. General Franco, watching from the VIP box, was reported to have greatly appreciated another victory over the forces of Communism.

In 1968, for the second successive tournament, the hosts – Italy, this time – ended up as champions. But the *Azzurri* struggled all the way. They even needed the toss of a coin to earn a place in the final after their semi against the Soviet Union finished goalless following extra-time – the penalty shoot-out was yet to be dreamed up.

In the other semi-final Yugoslavia beat England 1–0 in Florence in a match which was doubly disappointing for the World Cup holders, who were making their finals debut. Not only did they lose, but right-half Alan Mullery became the first senior England player to be sent off.

Yugoslavia, inspired by the left-wing skills of Dragan Dzajic, were given a better-than-evens chance of beating the pressure-frozen Italians in the final in Rome's Stadio Olimpico. Dzajic provided the Slavs with an early lead but Angelo Domenghini equalised controversially from a free-kick with 10 minutes remaining. The European Championship again saw extra-time fail to provide any more goals, so the final went to a replay, again in Rome. Yugoslavia resisted spiritedly in the opening minutes and protested furiously that Gigi Riva's opening goal, after 12 minutes, should have been disallowed for offside. But the hosts, once ahead, took control.

Pietro Anatasi, about to cost Juventus a then world record £500,000 from Varese, scored their second goal on the half hour. Italy were European champions for the first and, so far, only time.

THE TEAMS

The record books prove that it is 16 of Europe's most powerful nations who will contest the 2004 crown, including eight previous winners and eight previous hosts. Apart from the World Cup, it is hard to think of any other major international tournament that can boast as many strong teams. Every single one has a chance of winning matches and even the favourites are hardly likely to arrive in Portugal feeling immune from the possibility of shocks.

SPAIN, from Group A, were second winners in 1964 while **RUSSIA** inherited the mantle of the former Soviet Union who won the inaugural Nations Cup in 1960 and were then runners-up three times including 1964 when Spain played hosts.

PORTUGAL will join the pantheon of hosts the moment they kick off the finals on June 12 in Oporto against **GREECE**.

Group B brings together two heavyweights in **FRANCE** and **ENGLAND** with the French defending the crown they regained four years ago. Their previous success was in 1984 when they were hosts for the second time after the debut event of 1960. England staged the finals in 1996 but the crown itself has proved elusive. **SWITZERLAND** and **CROATIA** complete the group.

ITALY will command favourites' attention in Group C. Yet despite having been hosts twice, they won the title just the once, as hosts for the first time in 1968. Second time around, in 1980, Italy were fourth. Their single title is thus an achievement emulated by **DENMARK** in 1992 when their Nordic neighbours **SWEDEN** were hosts for the one and only time. **BULGARIA** are thus very much junior partners.

Group D boasts more past success than any other section. **GERMANY** (both as West Germany and then unified Germany) carried off the Henri Delaunay trophy a record three times, in 1972, 1980 and 1996, and hosted the event once – in 1988 when **HOLLAND**, co-hosts with Belgium four years ago, grabbed the glory for the one and only time so far.

The **CZECH REPUBLIC**, as Czechoslovakia, were winners in 1976 on the only occasion the final was decided by a penalty shoot-out.

At the other end of the achievement scale come **LATVIA**. They are the only newcomers to the finals but, as Turkey found out to their cost in the qualifying play-offs, certainly not opponents to underestimate.

THE REFEREES

Refereeing trios from the same country will be in charge of all matches in the finals. UEFA long ago abandoned the system of mixing up nationalities which FIFA uses, controversially, for the World Cup. So the 12 referees will be supported by 'proper' assistant referees from their own country. Four other referees have been nominated specifically for the role of fourth referee.

Star among the officials is the Italian Pierluigi Collina, who was in charge of the 2002 World Cup Final in Yokohama between Brazil and Germany and several high-tension Euro qualifiers – including the goalless draw between Turkey and England in Istanbul.

Markus Merk from Germany refereed the 2003 Champions League Final between Milan and Juventus in Manchester. Slovakia's Lubos Michel was in charge of the 2003 UEFA Cup Final between Porto and Celtic in Seville.

Michel and his assistants are one of two trios from non-finalist nations, the other coming from Norway and being led by Terje Hauge. Five of the finalists do not have any refereeing representation – Croatia, Bulgaria, Czech Republic, Latvia and Holland.

The Officials	
Denmark:	Kim Milton Nielsen (assistants Lens Larsen, Joergen Jepsen)
England:	Mike Riley (Philip Sharp, Glenn Turner)
France:	Gilles Veissière (Frederic Arnault, Serge Vallin)
Germany:	Markus Merk (Christian Schraer, Jan-Henrik Salver)
Italy:	Pierluigi Collina (Marco Ivaldi, Narciso Pisacreta)
Norway:	Terje Hauge (Steinar Holvik, Ole Hermann Borgan)
Portugal:	Lucilio Cardoso Cortez Batista (Paulo Jorge Januario Leite Ribeiro, Jose Manuel Silva Cardinal)
Russia:	Valentin Ivanov (Gennady Krasyuk, Vladimir Eniutin)
Slovakia:	Lubos Michel (Igor Sramka, Martin Balko)
Spain:	Manuel Enrique Mejuto González (Oscar Martinez, Rafael Guerrero)
Sweden:	Anders Frisk (Kenneth Petersson, Peter Ekstrom)
Switzerland:	Urs Meier (Francesco Buragina, Rudolf Kappeli)
Fourth officials:	Frank De Bleechere (Belgium), Kyros Vassaras (Greece), Alain Hamer (Luxembourg), Stuart Dougal (Scotland)

Above: Comrades in arms: Marco Delvecchio and
Luis Figo head off the pitch after last year's friendly

PORTUGAL

Brazil's World Cup-winning coach Luiz Felipe Scolari surprised a few people by arriving in Lisbon to sign up as boss and take charge of Portugal's under-achieving national team in December 2002. He is currently making no secret of his intention to win the European crown.

Scolari insists that Portugal, hosts of a major tournament for the first time, have the talent necessary to win their first senior trophy despite the humiliation of a first-round exit from the World Cup in South Korea and Japan.

"I haven't come here just to do a good job," he told the nation on arrival. "I have won titles in South America and Asia but I know it's also important to succeed in Europe, so this is a personal goal as well as an important appointment. I do not take teams into competitions not to win."

Scolari, well-travelled and educated in the ways and names of the international game, has done his video homework. But he also wasted no time in setting his personal stamp of authority on the job and in letting the senior players know who was in charge.

The issue was Scolari's inclusion of the FC Porto playmaker, Deco, in the squad within days of him having obtained Portuguese citizenship. Deco – real name Anderson Luis de Souza – has played virtually all his senior football in Portugal but his inclusion to make his debut in a friendly, against – of all people – Brazil, raised enormous controversy.

'Untouchables' such as Real Madrid's Luis Figo and Milan's Manuel Rui Costa grumbled that: "National anthems can be learned but they are not felt." But Scolari had an uncompromising reply, warning any would-be rebels: "I pick the team, not the players, and I don't give in to pressure from anyone. I am interested in quality players and Deco is a quality player. Anyone who disagrees doesn't have to turn up. No one is pointing a gun at anyone's head."

Deco did his own talking out on the pitch by scoring Portugal's winner in their 2–1 win over Brazil and, since then, Scolari has been left, unchallenged, to prepare for the decisive battles ahead.

Portugal's initial results under Scolari were patchy. In his 10 initial outings they beat opposition ranging from the extremes of Brazil and Norway on the one hand to Albania, Macedonia, Bolivia and Kazakhstan on the other. They drew with Holland and Paraguay but lost to Italy and Spain.

Scolari's challenge is to integrate the surviving members of the so-called 'golden generation' who won the World Youth Cup twice in 1989 and 1991 with the bright young things who have exploded on European football in the last few years. Veteran defender Fernando Couto, Rui Costa, Figo and Joao Pinto are the 'golden oldies', with the addition of Sergio Conceicao and new kids on the block such as Manchester United's Cristiano Ronaldo, Barcelona's Ricardo Quaresma, Newcastle's Hugo Viana and Tottenham's Helder Postiga.

The Portuguese have long been nicknamed 'the Brazilians of Europe' because of their matchless technique, short-passing style and ability to weave interminable patterns across the pitch. But fragile morale and lack of tactical discipline has often let them down. Traditionally, Portugal have used a 4-4-2 with a flat back four; Scolari is an advocate of 3-5-2, a system which can pay dividends at international level because it depends on a high level of player intelligence – not necessarily available to a club boss.

Scolari used a three-man defence to win the World Cup for Brazil and faces a challenge teaching the Portuguese national team new tricks. At least the fact that many of his players are with foreign clubs means they have a grasp of tactical variation to embellish their technique. In this Scolari is fortunate. As he says: "Spirit and aggression can be added to a player's game – what I cannot do is teach people who don't know how to play football. Our aim is to add something extra – which can turn Portugal into European champions."

Coach Luiz Felipe Scolari

The Portuguese federation sprung a surprise when they persuaded Brazil's 2002 World Cup-winning coach to take up the challenge of turning them, at last, into international winners. 'Big Phil' had a track record of success and reputation for instilling physical and tactical discipline into all his teams. He had won the South American club championship, the Copa Libertadores, with Gremio in 1995 and then again with Palmeiras in 1999. Later he bossed Gremio again and then Criciuma and Cruzeiro, before taking the Brazil job in June 2001 after the short-lived reigns of Wanderley Luxemburgo and Emerson Leao. Made an ideal start in Portugal by guiding his adopted national team to a 2–1 win over... Brazil.

Championship Record

2000	–	semi-finals
1996	–	quarter-finals
1992	–	did not qualify
1988	–	did not qualify
1984	–	semi-finals
1980	–	did not qualify
1976	–	did not qualify
1972	–	did not qualify
1968	–	did not qualify
1964	–	did not qualify
1960	–	quarter-finals

The Coach

Luiz Felipe Scolari, aged 55
(born September 11, 1948)

Star Performers

Ricardo (Ricardo Pereira)
Position: goalkeeper
Club: Sporting
Born: 11.2.1976

Sergio Conceicao
Position: midfield
Club: Lazio
Born: 15.11.1974

Luis Figo
Position: winger/midfield
Club: Real Madrid
Born: 4.11.1972

Cristiano Ronaldo
Position: winger
Club: Manchester United
Born: 5.2.1985

Pauleta (Pedro Resende)
Position: forward
Club: Paris Saint-Germain
Born: 28.4.1973

FERNANDO COUTO Aged 34 (born August 2, 1969). Lanky Couto began as a midfield anchor before settling into his career role in the heart of defence. He was a youth world champion with Portugal in 1989 and was promoted for his senior debut in 1–0 win over the United States a year later. Now with Lazio in Italy after highly successful spells with FC Porto and Parma with whom he won the UEFA Cup in 1995.

GREECE

Greece will be contesting the European finals for the second time in their history some 24 years after their first appearance in Italy back in 1980. On that occasion they crashed out in the opening round – as they did on their World Cup finals debut in 1994. In 2004, it could be different.

This time some of the most passionate and quickly aroused fans in European football expect better of the squad patiently built, despite all sorts of hurdles, by German coach Otto Rehhagel. Clubs such as Panathinaikos and AEK of Athens or Olympiakos from nearby Piraeus rank among the richest in Europe. But the power of the big clubs worked, for years, against the interests of the national team. The clubs were reluctant to release their players for internationals, and lack of preparation was reflected in regular failure in European and World Cup preliminaries.

The seeds for the latest Greek revival were sown in the disastrous season of 2000–01 which was interrupted by a players' strike in a row over refereeing standards, and then a squabble between the federation and the government over administrative changes and security.

That was the minefield into which veteran German coach Rehhagel walked in the summer of 2001. The Greek media was sceptical. A string of near-misses early in Rehhagel's coaching career had earned him the nickname of "Otto II" and he was widely considered to have taken the job to fill in between Bundesliga appointments.

Critics did not know their man. Rehhagel knew his international football. One of his first changes was to banish all the relatives, hangers-on and reporters from the national team camp. A second change was to persuade the federation to use as the squad's base a new training centre an hour's drive beyond Athens rather than the facilities of one of the big clubs. He then made sure his players knew who was boss by expelling from the national team the Hannover forward Kostas Konstantinidis after a touchline row during a game against Austria.

When the Euro 2004 qualifying draw was made, the best most Greek fans could hope for was finishing runners-up. Mighty Spain were top seeds. Pessimism was apparently justified when Greece lost 2–0 at home to Spain in their opening match.

But after losing their first two qualifying ties, Greece won all the next six, at home and away, conceding no more goals. Amazingly, a goal from Stelios Giannakopoulos secured a shock 1–0 win away to the Spaniards in Zaragoza.

Yet they qualified by scoring only eight goals, by far the lowest total of any of the group-winners. Statistics thus tell a tale of the Greeks' Achilles heel and three of those goals were scored by Angelos Haristeas from one of Rehhagel's old clubs, Werder Bremen. The most important goal, however, was the penalty converted by Vasilios Tsartas to beat Northern Ireland after a foul on Zisis Vryzas.

Tsartas, now home with AEK after a spell in Spain where his goals lifted Sevilla back into La Liga, is one of the most self-possessed of the Greek players. Other AEK players hold steady places in Rehhagel's squad along with Panathinaikos goalkeeper Antonis Nikopolidos, defender Yourkas Seitaridis and playmaker Angelos Basinas, as well as Olympiakos defenders Stelios Venetidis and Paraskevas Antzas, midfielders Giorgios Georgiadis and Stelios Giannakopoulos, now at Bolton Wanderers. But it is strikers Vryzas, Haristeas and Atletico Madrid's Demis Nikolaidis who must raise their game the highest in Portugal.

When Greece reached USA 94, then manager Altekas Panagulias said: "The dark days have ended for Greek soccer. We have not conquered the world merely by qualifying for the finals but I can safely say we have opened the door for worldwide recognition."

Sadly, the jury is still out.

Coach Otto Rehhagel

Rehhagel had his contract instantly extended to 2006 as soon as he guided Greece to these finals. Rehhagel was a versatile Bundesliga professional in the 1960s with Rot-Weiss Essen, Hertha Berlin and Kaiserslautern, scoring 22 goals in 201 games. Coaching proved his forte, particularly during two stints at Werder Bremen when he won the league twice, the cup twice and the 1992 Cup-Winners' Cup. Other clubs included Borussia Dortmund, Arminia Bielefeld, Fortuna Dusseldorf, Bayern Munich and Kaiserslautern – whom he led out of the second division to the league title. Rehhagel took up the Greek appointment in the summer of 2001.

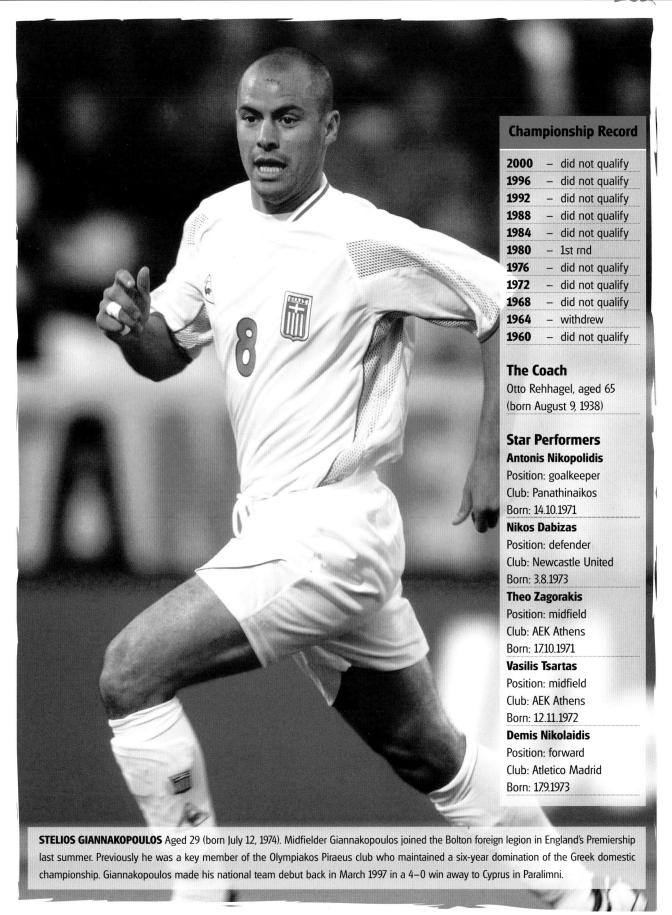

Championship Record

2000	– did not qualify
1996	– did not qualify
1992	– did not qualify
1988	– did not qualify
1984	– did not qualify
1980	– 1st rnd
1976	– did not qualify
1972	– did not qualify
1968	– did not qualify
1964	– withdrew
1960	– did not qualify

The Coach

Otto Rehhagel, aged 65
(born August 9, 1938)

Star Performers

Antonis Nikopolidis
Position: goalkeeper
Club: Panathinaikos
Born: 14.10.1971

Nikos Dabizas
Position: defender
Club: Newcastle United
Born: 3.8.1973

Theo Zagorakis
Position: midfield
Club: AEK Athens
Born: 17.10.1971

Vasilis Tsartas
Position: midfield
Club: AEK Athens
Born: 12.11.1972

Demis Nikolaidis
Position: forward
Club: Atletico Madrid
Born: 17.9.1973

STELIOS GIANNAKOPOULOS Aged 29 (born July 12, 1974). Midfielder Giannakopoulos joined the Bolton foreign legion in England's Premiership last summer. Previously he was a key member of the Olympiakos Piraeus club who maintained a six-year domination of the Greek domestic championship. Giannakopoulos made his national team debut back in March 1997 in a 4–0 win away to Cyprus in Paralimni.

SPAIN

Spain were the second winners of the European crown way back in 1964. But 40 bleak years since then have sent a chill wind of confusion swirling about the nation's status in the international game. Despite outstanding players, the club versus country dilemma could still undermine the cause.

Considering the talent of the men in the virbrant red shirt down the years, it is almost beyond belief that Spain have reached a major final on only one occasion other than 1964. That was in 1984, also in the European Championship, when a team weakened by injuries and suspensions lost 2–0 to their Platini-inspired French hosts.

Jorge Valdano, the Argentine sports director of Real Madrid, believes the club ethic in Spain has drowned out national pride. He says: "In South America kids grow up dreaming of playing for Brazil or Argentina or Uruguay. That's the peak of achievement. But in Spain kids grow up with the ultimate ambition of playing for Real Madrid or Barcelona or Bilbao. The balance is all wrong for the national team."

Tipping the balance the other way has proved a frustrating task for top bosses such as Ladislao Kubala, Miguel Munoz, Luis Suarez, Javier Clemente, Jose Antonio Camacho and now Inaki Saez. They have ensured Spain a regular presence at the big events but going beyond the quarter-finals appears impossible.

Four years ago Spain had the chance of taking favourites France to extra-time in their Euro quarter-final in Bruges. But then Real Madrid superstar Raul, of all people, missed a penalty and it was home again. Same story at the World Cup. Spain reached 'only' the quarter-finals and lost 5–3 to co-hosts South Korea in a shoot-out after a goalless draw.

The lack of big-occasion confidence was evident once more in the Euro qualifiers. Spain were in one of the easiest groups and made an ideal start with a 2–0 win away to Greece. But in the middle of the campaign Spain took their eye off the ball and lost 1–0 at home to Greece, followed by failure to win away to Northern Ireland. They ended up as runners-up and had to scramble past Norway in the play-offs.

Saez must have breathed a huge sigh of relief. He was under pressure to take Spain to the finals not merely because of fans' expectations but for all sorts of political reasons. First, Spain is next door to Portugal, so a failure to attend their neighbours' party would have been humiliating. Secondly, Portugal had already thrashed Spain in committee by an embarrassing margin to win hosting rights for the finals.

Now the hard work begins. Saez must bring his squad together after a season of ferocious inter-club rivalry and turn La Liga antagonists into team-mates unified in a single national purpose. The backbone of the team is obvious, starting with Real Madrid's Iker Casillas in goal. Still only 23, Casillas already has Champions and Spanish league honours to his name. Ahead of him, Casillas is offered protection by club-mate Michel Salgado at right-back. Sealing up the centre of defence will be Barcelona's Carles Puyol. Madrid's Ivan Helguera can play equally as well in central defence or as anchor man in midfield where Valeron – "the best passer in the world" according to French newspaper *L'Equipe* – pulls the strings.

Up front it's all down to the nimble genius of Raul and one of the new boys such as Sevilla's Jose Antonio Reyes or Atletico Madrid's raw but fast-learning Fernando Torres. Around them Saez is fortunate to have a clutch of up-and-coming talents such as Real Sociedad's Xabi Alonso, Depor's Alberto Luque and Valencia's Ruben Baraja and Vicente Rodriguez.

Indeed, perhaps Saez has too much talent. His challenge is getting the mix sorted. Then the timing is right for a Spanish revival. Spain were champions in 1964 and runners-up in 1984. Perhaps now, a further 20 years on, is an appropriate time to get it right once more.

Coach: Jose Ignacio 'Inaki' Saez

Saez, former right-back with Athletic Bilbao, was appointed originally as a stop-gap when World Cup boss Jose Camacho quit after Spain's exit to South Korea. Previously Saez had maintained the Spanish tradition for outstanding youth coaches – guiding Spain to victory in the 1998 European U-21 Championship and the juniors to success in the World Under-17 Cup a year later. Saez played three times for Spain in the late 1960s, then stayed on with Bilbao after retiring to work his way up the coaching ladder. Saez became boss of Bilbao and then had spells with Las Palmas and Albacete before joining the federation coaching staff in 1996.

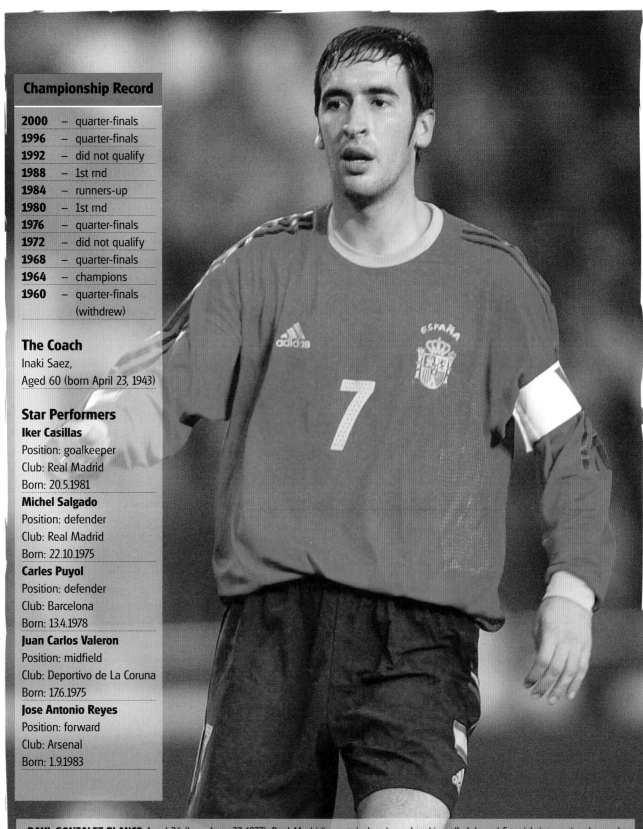

Championship Record

2000	–	quarter-finals
1996	–	quarter-finals
1992	–	did not qualify
1988	–	1st rnd
1984	–	runners-up
1980	–	1st rnd
1976	–	quarter-finals
1972	–	did not qualify
1968	–	quarter-finals
1964	–	champions
1960	–	quarter-finals (withdrew)

The Coach
Inaki Saez,
Aged 60 (born April 23, 1943)

Star Performers
Iker Casillas
Position: goalkeeper
Club: Real Madrid
Born: 20.5.1981

Michel Salgado
Position: defender
Club: Real Madrid
Born: 22.10.1975

Carles Puyol
Position: defender
Club: Barcelona
Born: 13.4.1978

Juan Carlos Valeron
Position: midfield
Club: Deportivo de La Coruna
Born: 17.6.1975

Jose Antonio Reyes
Position: forward
Club: Arsenal
Born: 1.9.1983

RAUL GONZALEZ BLANCO Aged 26 (born June 27, 1977). Real Madrid's captain has been breaking all club and Spanish international records since making his league debut at 17. He has won the Champions League three times but has a Euro finals score to settle after missing a crucial quarter-final penalty against France in 2000. Typically, Raul turned up trumps in the Norway play-off with goals in both legs.

RUSSIA

When Russia crashed chaotically out of the last World Cup even their own players wrote off their chances of reaching Portugal. But under the inspired leadership of Georgi Yartsev, the team overcame a poor start in the Euro 2004 qualifiers to come through after a play-off against Wales.

Russia struggled through the first half of the Euro 2004 qualifiers. Valeri Gazzayev had succeeded Oleg Romantsev as coach after the World Cup, but he grew increasingly irritated with the restrictions of being national manager and quit last August after a 2–1 home defeat by Israel in a friendly. "That was a shameful, disgusting performance by our team," raged Gazzayev. "The players lack any will to win."

The facts bore out his frustration. Russia had taken only one point from their previous three qualifying ties in Group 10 against Albania, Georgia and Switzerland. They were third in the table, three points behind the Irish Republic in second place and five adrift of leaders Switzerland.

The federation, reluctantly, accepted Gazzayev's resignation. Then, running out of managerial candidates, they brought former Moscow Spartak boss Georgi Yartsev out of semi-retirement.

Yartsev's immediate challenge was to reconstruct a shattered team inside a fortnight to withstand an Irish onslaught in Dublin. He did not hesitate to put his faith in experience. Back, in midfield, came Celta Vigo's Alexander Mostovoi and FC Porto's Dmitri Alenichev with veteran central defender Victor Onopko reinstated as captain. Two wins and a draw later and Russia had secured runners-up spot in the group to earn a two-leg qualifying play-off against Wales.

Yartsev, who knew Alenichev from their time together as coach and player at Spartak, also went back to their old club to recall playmaker Yegor Titov while also calling up unheralded striker Dmitry Bulykin from Moscow Dynamo. Bulykin rose to the occasion with a hat-trick in only his second international, a 4–1 win over ultimate group winners Switzerland.

Russian football has never been about scintillating attack. Only in the mid-1970s and 1980s did the Soviet Union side earn plaudits for its attacking invention. After *Glasnost*, Russia reverted to the unimaginative football reminiscent of the Moscow-dominated teams of the 1950s and 1960s. Throwback football was what Russia produced in the goalless first leg of the play-off in Moscow. They were far happier in Cardiff, hitting Wales clinically on the break to win 1–0. The drawback to Yartsev's success lay in raising expectations for the finals. Yartsev may struggle to persuade his countrymen to restrict their dreams of Russian achievement.

The old, Russia-dominated Soviet Union won the inaugural European Championship – then called the Nations Cup – back in 1960 with a team starring the legendary goalkeeper Lev Yashin. They were runners-up to Spain in 1964, semi-finalists in 1968 and runners-up again both in 1972 to West Germany and then in 1988 to Holland. But the days when Russia were considered as anything better than first-round failures at a major tournament have long gone.

Yartsev will rely on the old recipe which revived Russia. That almost certainly starts with Lokomotiv's Sergei Ovchinnikov in goal. Yevseyev and the old warhorse Onopko, now playing back in Russia with Alaniya Vladikavkaz, will take few prisoners in defence. But much depends on how Russia's unpredictable playmakers adjust to the Portuguese pressure.

Mostovoi is the most moody of all. He was fined by his Spanish club, Celta, for vanishing back to Russia for too long to celebrate the victory over Wales. Dmitri Loskov of Lokomotiv and Alexei Smertin – on loan to Portsmouth from Chelsea this past season – underline the depth of ability in midfield. But Russia will need Marseille's Dmitri Sychev at his best in attack if all the hopes raised by Yartsev's rescue act are to be fulfilled.

Coach **Georgi Alexandrovich Yartsev**

Yartsev faced an apparently hopeless task when he succeeded Valeri Gazzayev last August with Russia third in their group. But in six weeks he inspired two wins and a draw to earn the play-off place leading to victory over Wales. Yartsev, who won five caps in attack for the Soviet Union, had previously coached Moscow Spartak and Rotor Volgograd. He recalled several scapegoats from the first-round flop at the 2002 World Cup and revived morale to decisive effect. Yartsev's success quelled media demands for a foreign manager. His aides are ex-internationals in Alexander Borodyuk, Igor Chugainov and one-time World Cup goalkeeper Rinat Dassayev.

Championship Record

2000	– did not qualify
1996	– 1st rnd

As the Commonwealth of Independent States:

1992	– 1st rnd

As the Soviet Union:

1988	– runners-up
1984	– did not qualify
1980	– did not qualify
1976	– quarter-finals
1972	– runners-up
1968	– fourth place
1964	– runners-up
1960	– champions

The Coach

Georgi Alexandrovich Yartsev, aged 56 (born April 11, 1948)

Star Performers

Sergei Ovchinnikov
Position: goalkeeper
Club: Lokomotiv Moscow
Born: 10.11.1970

Vadim Yevseyev
Position: defender
Club: Lokomotiv Moscow
Born: 8.1.1976

Alexander Mostovoi
Position: midfield
Club: Celta Vigo
Born: 22.8.1968

Dmitri Sychev
Position: forward
Club: Marseille
Born: 26.10.1983

Dmitri Bulykin
Position: striker
Club: Moscow Dynamo
Born: 20.11.1979

VIKTOR ONOPKO Aged 34 (born October 14, 1969). The veteran at the heart of Russia's defence probably thought his international career was over after the 2002 World Cup. But reinstatement has rewarded the return to form of one of the last Russian players to have made his original international debut back at the turn of the 1990s for the former Soviet Union. Onopko is a veteran of the 1992 European finals.

GREAT MOMENTS FROM THE PAST

Playing great football, Franz Beckenbauer and Co open up a new era of German domination as the Soviets slide in Brussels... the first-ever penalty shoot-out brings surprise success for the Czechoslovaks in Belgrade when they beat the invincible Germans at their own game... then the great Karl-Heinz Rummenigge fires Germany back into command of the European game as Italy become host nation for the second time but fail to take the title.

Italy's title defence in 1972 was brought to an abrupt end in the quarter-finals by Belgium whose reward was to host the finals of what was now known, formally, as the European Championship.

Favourites were West Germany whose manager, Helmut Schoen, had built a spectacular new team around a nucleus of stars from Bayern Munich and Borussia Moenchengladbach, including Franz Beckenbauer, Gunter Netzer and record marksman Gerd Muller. The Germans underlined their power by beating England 3–1 at Wembley in the quarter-finals.

The semi-final draw split the last four evenly between eastern and western Europe. Anderlecht's Parc Astrid saw the Soviet Union defeat Hungary 1–0, while Antwerp witnessed West Germany defeat hosts Belgium 2–1.

Beckenbauer and his team were clear favourites to win the final in the Heysel Stadium in Brussels. The new, improved Soviet Union duly proved no match for this German side. Netzer dominated midfield and hit a post before two typically opportunist strikes from Muller and another from Herbert Wimmer decided the match. The 3–0 scoreline remains the largest winning margin of any European Championship final.

Muller finished as the tournament's 11-goal top scorer, with more than twice as many goals as the joint runners-up: East Germany's Hans Kreische, England's Martin Chivers, Holland's Johan Cruyff and Piet Keizer each scored five goals. With 16 goals, Muller was by now the leading marksman in the history of the European Championship.

The Germans had been outstanding winners but the 1976 finals were even more dramatic in that all the matches went to extra-time. Ultimate winners were the outsiders from Czechoslovakia who had made an awful start by losing their opening qualifier 3–0 to England at Wembley.

Above: Back where they belong? Horst Hrubesch and Manny Kaltz of West Germany hold aloft the European Nations trophy after beating the Soviet Union 3–0

Right: Der Bomber and Der Kaiser: Gerd Muller and Franz Beckenbauer celebrate the number 13's strike against the Soviet Union as coach Helmut Schoen's hugely talented side win 3–0 to lay the foundations of a lengthy period of German domination of the European game

Yugoslavia hosted the finals in which the Czechoslovaks defeated much fancied Holland 3–1 in extra-time. The Dutch finished with nine men after referee Clive Thomas sent off midfielders Johan Neeskens and Wim Van Hanegem. The other semi saw West Germany hit back from 2–0 down to beat Yugoslavia 4–2. The Germans had found a new Muller – Dieter Muller from Cologne. He scored a hat-trick against Yugoslavia and led the German fightback in the final after they had gone 2–0 down in 25 minutes to Czechoslovakia. One minute remained in normal time when Bernd Holzenbein's equaliser sent the game into extra-time.

No more goals came and extra-time ended amid chaos. The federations had agreed the previous day that, in the event of a draw, the match – and the championship – would be decided by a new-fangled penalty shoot-out. Oddly, the Czechoslovak players, however, had no knowledge of this. As defender Koloman Gogh explained later: "When extra-time ended we were all heading for the dressing rooms when we were waved back. We didn't know what was going on."

After penalty practice in training, the Czechoslovaks proved to be the better prepared. Masny opened up for Czechoslovakia, Rainer Bonhof equalised; Nehoda scored, Heinz Flohe levelled; Ondrus converted, Hannes Bongartz squared it; Jurkemik made no mistake, Uli Hoeness shot... over the bar. Panenka strolled up for the next kick, dummied one way, sending Maier in the wrong direction, and chipped the ball gently over him.

Czechoslovakia were champions of Europe not with a galaxy of stars but thanks to disciplined teamwork honed and perfected to such a degree by Voclav Jezek and assistant Jozef Venglos that they had gone 21 matches without defeat... since that 3–0 beating by England with which they started the European Championship campaign.

The tournament was so popular that UEFA doubled the size of the finals in 1980 to eight countries split into two groups. On one side hosts Italy were grouped with England, Belgium and Spain, while the other section featured old rivals West Germany and Holland, holders Czechoslovakia and newcomers Greece.

A place direct into the final was the reward for topping each group. England's hopes dipped after a 1–0 defeat by Italy for whom Marco Tardelli struck an 80th-minute winner. But Italy were pipped to top spot by Belgium. The other group saw Germany progress on a 1–0 revenge victory over Czechoslovakia, a 3–2 win over Holland – inspired by Bernd Schuster – and a goalless draw with Greece.

The Germans had a new hero in striker Karl-Heinz Rummenigge who climaxed the final by providing the corner from which Horst Hrubesch headed a last-minute winner. The Germans thus edged to a 2–1 victory over Belgium. Hrubesch had also scored the Germans' first goal in the 10th minute. The Belgians had levelled – briefly – through Rene Vandereycken's 72nd-minute penalty.

SWITZERLAND

Switzerland have reached the finals of the World Cup seven times, but Euro 2004 will be only their second appearance in the finals of the European Championship. The Swiss campaign will be watched with particular interest by many in the game – because they co-host Euro 2008.

Right now, Swiss football is on the up. At club level Basel have proved the point with their Champions League ambitions, while domestic passions have been revived by the ambitious stadia-building projects set under way by the federation and state authorities.

But building a team worthy of fulfilling all those hopes and dreams is another matter. Two national coaches stand out in Swiss history. One was Karl Rappan in the 1940s and 1950s; the other was Englishman Roy Hodgson who guided the Swiss to their Euro finals debut in England in 1996.

Now the legacy has been picked up by former international midfielder 'Kobi' Kuhn. Remarkably, he took the Swiss to the top of qualifying Group 10 ahead of Russia and the experienced Republic of Ireland, but the ride was anything but straightforward.

After missing the qualifying boat for the 2002 World Cup, Switzerland appeared in disarray at the start of preliminaries for the European Championship. The previous spring, Kuhn had banished experienced stars such as central defender Stephane Henchoz, anchor Ciri Sforza and centre-forward Stephane Chapuisat from the squad after accusing them of undermining morale. In due course Henchoz and Chapuisat were admitted back into the ranks, but Kuhn had made his point and the squad's new-found harmony was a decisive factor in the progress towards Portugal.

Bayern Munich's coach Ottmar Hitzfeld was among an impressed audience, saying: "Switzerland are one of the best-organised teams around. They have a clear tactical concept, they play neat football, they make the most of their own chances and restrict the opposition to as few as possible."

That recipe brought qualifying victories at home to Georgia, Albania and Ireland and away to Ireland and only one defeat. But that defeat, by 4–1 in Russia, very nearly derailed the Swiss in sight of their goal.

In the run-up to the decisive final match at home to Ireland, the greatest uncertainty for Kuhn concerned the form and fitness of Hakan Yakin, younger of the two brothers from Basel. Yakin duly proclaimed himself fit to face Ireland and scored the opening goal after only six minutes. Alex Frei, who helped create that goal, grabbed the decisive second himself on the hour. Switzerland's 2–0 win was the perfect present for Kuhn, who celebrated his 60th birthday the following day.

Half a dozen of Kuhn's squad are drawn from the outstanding Basel side built by Christian Gross. These include reserve goalkeeper Pascal Zuberbuhler, defenders Murat Yakin and Marco Zwyssig and midfielders Hakan Yakin, Benjamin Huggel and Marco Streller. Finding the best mix between the stars of Basel and the 'foreign legion' has paid dividends. Yet only three of the exports are with leading clubs – defenders Henchoz (Liverpool) and Patrick Muller (Lyon) and midfielder Fabio Celestini (Marseille).

Indeed several national team-mates have been playing lower division football such as defenders Bernt Haas in England with West Bromwich and Bruno Berner in Germany with Freiburg. Johann Vogel (PSV Eindhoven), Raphael Wicky (Hamburg) and Frei (Rennes), too, are solid pros rather than stars. But this need not be a drawback. As Vogel, a teenage Euro debutant in England in 1996, says: "The big tournaments are windows for any player to showcase his ability and, hopefully, earn a transfer up the ladder. It's a great incentive." Veteran striker Chapuisat knows all about the springboard effect. He led the Swiss attack at Euro 96 and won a Champions League final with Borussia Dortmund against Juventus. As he says: "There is much more to us than people think."

Coach Jakob 'Kobi' Kuhn

Kuhn was Swiss football's pin-up of the 1960s. A creative attacking midfielder, he won six league titles and five domestic cups in more than 500 appearances with FC Zurich. Given his later ruthless treatment of stars who stepped out of line, it was ironic that he was dropped from Switzerland's first match at the 1966 World Cup finals in England after skipping the squad's hotel curfew. Kuhn retired after scoring five goals in 64 internationals and had one spell in charge of FC Zurich. He then spent most of his coaching years in charge of the national youth and Under-21s before being asked to succeed Enzo Trossero in June 2001. Kuhn was the first Swiss to coach the national team in 11 years.

Championship Record

2000	– did not qualify
1996	– 1st rnd
1992	– did not qualify
1988	– did not qualify
1984	– did not qualify
1980	– did not qualify
1976	– did not qualify
1972	– did not qualify
1968	– did not qualify
1964	– did not qualify
1960	– did not enter

The Coach
Jakob 'Kobi' Kuhn, aged 60 (born October 12, 1943)

Star Performers

Jorg Stiel
Position: goalkeeper
Club: Borussia M'gladbach
Born: 3.3.1968

Stephane Henchoz
Position: defender
Club: Liverpool
Born: 7.9.1974

Johann Vogel
Position: midfield
Club: PSV Eindhoven
Born: 8.3.1977

Alexandre Frei
Position: forward
Club: Rennes (France)
Born: 15.7.1979

Stephane Chapuisat
Position: forward
Club: Young Boys
Born: 28.6.1969

HAKAN YAKIN Aged 27 (born February 22, 1977). Yakin is the younger of two brothers from Basel (along with centre-back Murat Yakin) who have helped spark the revivals of both club and country. Hakan Yakin returned just in time from serious injury to score a decisive goal against the Irish Republic in their last qualifying tie. Marked his Swiss debut with a goal in a 4–1 win away to Oman in February 2000.

CROATIA

A new generation has brought a new challenge to Croatia as they return to the European finals in which they reached the last eight on their competitive international debut in 1996. Then they were fired up by wartime national pride, but could there be a peace dividend this time?

In 1996, wily old coach Miroslav Blazevic was fortunate to possess a nucleus developed in the former Yugoslavia. Players such as Davor Suker, Zvonimir Boban and Robert Prosinecki already possessed a wealth of experience and skill. Those, allied to the nationalistic pride burgeoning from a newly freed nation, proved a potent mix.

Croatia were third at the 1998 World Cup but that was the peak of the 'old' team's achievement. They missed out on Euro 2000, then failed to progress beyond the first round at the last World Cup despite victory over Italy.

Blazevic's nominated successor, Mirko Jozic, quit on the flight home and the federation turned to Otto Baric, a Croat who had spent most of his coaching career in Austria and Germany. Baric had twice taken teams to European club finals – Rapid Vienna in the 1985 Cup-Winners' Cup and Austria Salzburg in the 1994 UEFA Cup.

But rebuilding a national team was a new experience. Baric had precious little breathing space before the Euro qualifiers. Not surprisingly, Croatia started badly. A home goalless draw against minnows Estonia and 2–0 defeat in Bulgaria placed early question marks against Baric's work. Fortunately the winter break was followed by a 4–0 thrashing of Belgium and the Croat campaign was back on track.

Ultimately they beat group-winners Bulgaria 1–0 in their last match, earning them a play-off against Slovenia where Dado Prso came into his own. The Monaco striker had earned great acclaim with his Champions League exploits and he followed up by scoring both the Croat goals in their narrow two-leg victory over their Balkan neighbours. Prso was thrilled. Harking back to the spirit of Euro 96, he saw this as more than a football victory, saying: "I have seen my country in wartime. We went on playing football even when bombs and shells were falling. Fear, pain, fighting, bloodshed. That's no life. I am proud to play for my country in peacetime. Beating Slovenia was a wonderful Christmas present for our country."

Almost all of Baric's squad play abroad. Indeed, few of the European finalists will have to gather their players from so many other countries. Croatia's finest play their club football in Austria, Belgium, England, Germany, Israel, Italy, Switzerland and Ukraine.

Baric varies his tactics according to the opposition and the occasion. For the finals, he is likely to deploy a five-man midfield. German-based Mario Dabic (Leverkusen) and Jurica Vranjes (Stuttgart) can earn a host of new admirers for their tireless efforts in relaying the ball from defence to attack. Italian-based Dario Simic (Milan) and Igor Tudor (Juventus) bring all the ruthless discipline of Serie A to the defence, though Tudor's availability at the finals is restricted after he was sent off against Slovenia.

Up front Baric has a variety of players from whom to choose according to his tactical preference. Portsmouth's Ivica Mornar can play wide or up front, Olic is always a danger 'in the hole', while Prso needs his mid-season magic to carry all the way through to Portugal.

Baric has not given up hope of finding new talent to maintain competition for places. He says: "I decided right from the start I would count on 70 to 80 per cent of the players from the last World Cup. It's a strong squad but I always try to watch as many players as possible.

"We are not one of the favourites but it is only a handful of matches in a short space of time with no easy matches. Even nations like Germany and England now have problems outplaying smaller sides. Football is getting tougher and more competitive all the time. We are playing our part."

Coach Otto Baric

Baric took on a weighty challenge when, after the 2002 World Cup finals, he accepted the job from Croat legend Miroslav Blazevic. An average player, Baric was quickly recognised as a tactician and motivator after switching from player to coach with Lokomotiv Zagreb. His reputation quickly spread to Austria where he was a winner with Wacker Innsbruck and Linz ASK. Baric returned home with Zagreb and Dinamo Vinkovici, while simultaneously guiding Yugoslavia's amateurs to the now-defunct European title. More trophy-winning spells followed in Austria, Germany, Croatia and Turkey. Baric also had a short spell as Austria's national boss.

Championship Record

2000 – did not qualify
1996 – quarter-finals
1960-92 – did not exist

The Coach
Otto Baric, aged 60
(born June 19, 1933)

Star Performers
Stipe Pletikosa
Position: goalkeeper
Club: Shakhtar Donetsk
Born: 8.1.1979

Igor Tudor
Position: defender
Club: Juventus
Born: 16.4.1978

Dario Simic
Position: defender
Club: Milan
Born: 12.11.1975

Ivica Mornar
Position: forward
Club: Portsmouth
Born: 12.1.1974

Ivica Olic
Position: forward
Club: CSKA Moscow
Born: 14.9.1979

DADO PRSO Aged 29 (born November 5, 1974). Monaco striker Prso did not make his debut for Croatia until the spring of 2003, but then the year just went on getting better. In a sensational fortnight last November, he notched four Champions League goals in an 8–3 win over Deportivo, and then scored Croatia's goals, both home and away, which earned their Euro play-off triumph over Balkan rivals Slovenia.

FRANCE

France have been to the equivalent of football hell and back since they snatched Euro glory from the jaws of defeat, beating Italy in the 2000 final in Rotterdam's Feyenoord stadium. But the reigning World and European champions failed to notch a single goal in the 2002 World Cup.

The French could do no wrong a few years ago. World Cup-holders and Euro 2000 champions, they had legions of admirers worldwide, alongside a queue of foreign officials outside their Clairefontaine training centre trying to discover the secret of this French revolution. It was not only that France won their matches, it was that they did so playing amazing football generated by some of the world's greatest players.

Then it all went wrong. When coach Roger Lemerre took his squad to the 2002 World Cup finals in Korea and Japan they were cocooned in their own complacency. Disaster occurred. France crashed sensationally in the opening match to newcomers Senegal, and were eliminated in the first round, the first holders to crash out without scoring a single goal.

Lemerre was forced to resign. Sensibly, this time, the federation looked beyond the Clairefontaine 'mafia' and appointed Jacques Santini who had just guided Lyon to the first league title win in their history.

Santini is a big man in every sense, and this was a big job – rebuilding both team and morale. The success with which he achieved his twin goals are evident from France's unique record in qualifying from Group One. *Les Bleus* were the only team to win all their eight matches. They scored more goals, 29, than any other team; they conceded fewer goals, two, than any other team; and they achieved a greater gap (10 points) over their group runners-up (Slovenia) than any other country.

France were also the first nation to secure their finals tickets from the qualifiers. They spread their goals around the team. Juventus' David Trezeguet plus the Arsenal duo of Thierry Henry and Sylvain Wiltord scored six goals apiece, with Zinedine Zidane contributing three.

The backbone of the team will be easily recognizable. Fabien Barthez continues as first choice in goal despite his erratic spell in the Premiership with Manchester United. His wish to return to French football with Marseille was part-triggered by his own concern for his France place. The Lyon keeper, Gregory Coupet, for example, had proved an excellent deputy during last summer's Confederations Cup success.

Three-quarters of the World Cup-winning unit remain on duty in defence. Thuram and Bayern Munich's Bixente Lizarazu are first-choice for the wing-back roles, alongside France's most-capped player Marcel Desailly. Laurent Blanc having retired and Frank Leboeuf having decamped to Qatar, the increasingly impressive Mikael Silvestre has taken over as Desailly's central defensive partner. He continues to repel challenges from the likes of Auxerre's young hero, Philippe Mexes.

Zidane, despite the pressures of life at Real Madrid, remains the fulcrum in midfield. His wonderful sleight of foot, unerring passing accuracy and thunderous shot are crucial. That much was underlined by France's World Cup disaster when Zidane missed the first two games through injury.

Santini has a clutch of hard-working midfielders – Patrick Vieira, Olivier Dacourt, Benoit Pedretti – eager to win the ball for Zidane. He is also fortunate to be over-subscribed with striking talent. Trezeguet and Henry, for all their talent and pedigree, must stay sharp to withstand the rise of Djibril Cisse and Sidney Govou. Santini has released the brake and given the players the green light to express their attacking instincts.

But France are not perfect. No fewer than seven of Santini's main men are the wrong side of 30: Barthez, Thuram, Desailly, Lizarazu and Zidane plus Wiltord and Robert Pires. In a time-tight tournament, they may just find that the qualities of age and experience also have their drawbacks.

Coach Jacques Santini

Santini took over after *Les Bleus* had crashed out of the 2002 World Cup finals. Santini gained his authority from playing success in midfield with Saint-Etienne in the 1970s and then by guiding Lyon to the league title in 2002. He rejected demands for a totally new start, preferring to instil change by stealth as he integrated a string of promising newcomers. That softly softly approach was vindicated by results. France achieved a 100 per cent dash through the European qualifiers, while also winning the 2003 Confederation Cup.

Championship Record

2000	– champions
1996	– semi-finals
1992	– 1st rnd
1988	– did not qualify
1984	– champions (H)
1980	– did not qualify
1976	– did not qualify
1972	– did not qualify
1968	– quarter-finals
1964	– quarter-finals
1960	– semi-finals (4th, H)

The Coach

Jacques Santini, aged 52
(born April 25, 1952)

Star Performers

Lilian Thuram
Position: defender
Club: Juventus
Born: 1.1.1972

Marcel Desailly
Position: defender
Club: Chelsea
Born: 7.9.1968

Patrick Vieira
Position: midfield
Club: Arsenal
Born: 23.6.1976

David Trezeguet
Position: striker
Club: Juventus
Born: 15.10.1977

Thierry Henry
Position: striker
Club: Arsenal
Born: 17.8.1977

ZINEDINE ZIDANE Aged 31 (born June 23, 1972). Playmaker Zidane has generally been considered the world's finest footballer over the past six years – since he scored two of the French goals which sank Brazil in the 1998 World Cup Final. The former Cannes, Bordeaux and Juventus hero cost Real Madrid a world record £45million in 2001. He made his France debut in a 2–2 draw against the Czech Republic in August 1994.

ENGLAND

England will be one of the favourites for Euro 2004 – if they can field their strongest team. Sven-Goran Eriksson's squad topped Group Seven to qualify for the finals. They were unbeaten in all eight matches. But the memory of the 2002 World Cup continues to haunt them.

Right-back Gary Neville and midfield powerhouse Steven Gerrard both missed the last World Cup finals through injury. Their two world-class talents, David Beckham and Michael Owen, played despite lacking full fitness. Neville, a veteran with more than 50 caps, says: "If the core of the team stays fit, we have a real chance at Euro 2004. We have the quality and the age of the team is right. This is the most exciting England team that I've been part of. We've proved what a good side we are when everyone's fit, by beating Turkey in the qualifiers even though they finished third in the World Cup."

Yet Neville fears that the intensity of the Premiership makes England more vulnerable to knocks than most of their rivals. He said: "It seems as if every England squad is dominated by who's not there and who's injured."

England have never reached a European championship final. The closest they came was at home in Euro 96, when they lost on penalties to Germany in the semi-final. Euro 2000 was another disappointment.

England showed potential in the World Cup finals, but Eriksson has long claimed that his squad would not start to reach their peak until Euro 2004. They looked lethargic at times in qualifying. They fell behind in both games against Slovakia and Macedonia. They were unconvincing against Liechtenstein but saved their best displays for the crunch games against Turkey. Eriksson is not known for gambling. But he risked emerging teenager Wayne Rooney against the Turks at Sunderland and the Everton youngster galvanised England.

England gave their most impressive display in Istanbul, to clinch the point they needed. Their preparations had been chaotic. The squad threatened to strike and boycott the match after Manchester United centre-back Rio Ferdinand was excluded from selection by the Football Association for failing to take a drugs test.

They relented after lengthy discussions, then showed great team spirit to hold the Turks

comfortably. In Owen's absence, Rooney led Turkey's defence a merry dance. Beckham radiated confidence despite a bizarre penalty miss. Ferdinand's replacement John Terry was immense alongside Sol Campbell. Goalkeeper David James said: "It was top defending and a pleasure to be in goal behind them."

England have the players. Campbell and Ferdinand emerged from the World Cup with huge credit. Terry is one for the future. Nicky Butt may not be a regular for Manchester United but he is one of the best 'sitting' midfielders in international football. Gerrard may have finally solved the long-standing problem on the left of England's midfield diamond.

Beckham has grown even stronger since moving to Real Madrid and being given the chance to play in the centre of midfield. Owen is one of the world's great strikers. Rooney is a phenomenon. In Istanbul, he answered questions about his temperament too.

Question marks remain. Is James ready for the finals after playing the season with relegated West Ham in Division One? Is left-back Ashley Cole defensively solid enough at the highest level? Have Paul Scholes's goals from midfield dried up because of the counter-attacking tactics that Eriksson employs?

In the qualifiers, England gave mediocre opposition a one-goal start and recovered. They cannot afford that luxury in Portugal. In the end though, fit bodies will be crucial. If England can field their strongest team, they may take some holding.

Coach Sven-Goran Eriksson

England's first foreign coach divides media and fans. Detractors claim he lacks passion and point to England's second-half display in their World Cup defeat by Brazil. His admirers point to England's record in competitive games. That defeat by the World Cup-winners was their only loss in 19 matches under the Swede. His team set a record of eight consecutive wins, better than Sir Alf Ramsey's World Cup-winning side. Eriksson's style is low-key but not rigid. It is a style which brought Eriksson great success with IFK Gothenburg, Benfica and Lazio.

Championship Record

2000	–	1st rnd
1996	–	semi-finals (H)
1992	–	1st rnd
1988	–	1st rnd
1984	–	did not qualify
1980	–	1st rnd
1976	–	did not qualify
1972	–	quarter-finals
1968	–	semi-finals (3rd)
1964	–	did not enter
1960	–	did not enter

The Coach

Sven-Goran Eriksson, aged 56
(born February 9, 1948)

Star Performers

Sol Campbell
Position: defender
Club: Arsenal
Born: 18.9.1974

Paul Scholes
Position: midfield
Club: Manchester United
Born: 16.11.1974

David Beckham
Position: midfield
Club: Real Madrid
Born: 2.5.1975

Wayne Rooney
Position: striker
Club: Everton
Born: 24.10.1985

Michael Owen
Position: striker
Club: Liverpool
Born: 14.12.1979

STEVEN GERRARD Aged 24 (born May 30, 1980). Midfielder Gerrard has made such rapid progress that he was appointed to the captaincy of his home-town club, Liverpool, last autumn. Long-striding Gerrard made his England debut in a 2–0 win over Ukraine in May 2000. He played once at the subsequent European finals, but injury unluckily prevented him from lining up for England at the 2002 World Cup.

GREAT MOMENTS FROM THE PAST

Captain Platini leads with his goals and by example as fabulous France demonstrate a seismic shift in the balance of European footballing power and make the championship founder's dream come true in Paris... then it's the triumph of Total Football as Ruud Gullit and Marco van Basten's flying Dutchmen strike in style to make their long-overdue mark in Munich. They prove themselves one of the greatest teams ever seen on a football pitch.

France were not only hosts but also outstanding winners in 1984 – hinting at the strength in depth which would produce even greater successes in the late 1990s. This time around they owed success to the midfield trio of hard-working Luis Fernandez and Jean Tigana plus effervescent little Alain Giresse... topped off by the attacking genius of Michel Platini.

Denmark's emergence in the finals pointed to a new balance of power within Europe. The Danes had reached the finals by winning their qualifying group in magnificent fashion and courtesy of a 1–0 win over England at Wembley. Former European Footballer of the Year Allan Simonsen converted the crucial penalty. Unfortunately, injury hampered Denmark's prospects in the finals, which they opened with a 1–0 defeat by France, during which Simonsen broke his leg.

Platini was the match-winner with the first of his nine goals in five games. His haul included hat-tricks against Belgium and Yugoslavia, a last-minute of extra-time winner in the semi-final against Portugal, and the first goal of the final itself against Spain.

The Spaniards drew with Romania and Portugal but then beat a lacklustre West German side to top the other group. Loss of the European crown cost West German coach Jupp Derwall his job.

No such problems for Spanish boss Miguel Munoz as his men went on to edge Denmark in a penalty shoot-out in their semi-final in Lyon.

However, against France in the final, Spain's luck ran out. Injuries and suspensions played havoc with coach Munoz's tactical plan before an uncharacteristic slip by goalkeeper-captain Luis Arconada, after 56 minutes, proved decisive. Arconada, latest in a long line of outstanding Basque goalkeepers, allowed Platini's low drive from a free-kick to spin through his grasp and over the goal-line. Spain were doomed. France even overcame the sending-off of Yvon Le Roux after 84 minutes to score a second in the final minute, but their lead had never been seriously threatened.

France were not the only nation for whom European Championship success had proved elusive. The same could have been said of Holland, World Cup runners-up in 1974 and 1978. But in 1988, in West Germany, the Dutch finally secured the major prize which their pre-eminence in the international game should long since have earned.

Holland's victory over the Soviet Union in the 1988 final in Munich's Olympiastadion was serious evidence in favour of the Dutch approach to youth coaching and to all aspects of general football intelligence.

For the first event in three, the format was not changed. A qualifying section of mini-leagues was climaxed by two four-team groups in the finals, two direct elimination semi-finals and then the final itself.

In the qualifying round Italy, the Soviet Union, England and Holland swept all before them in their respective groups. Spain, Denmark and the Republic of Ireland – qualifying for the finals of a major tournament for the first time – all won through after a tight scrap.

The only hitch in the qualifying process occurred in Holland's home match against Cyprus on October 28, 1987. The Dutch won 8–0 but the result was later declared invalid by UEFA because a firework thrown from the crowd struck Cyprus goalkeeper Andreas Charitou. A replay was ordered which Holland also won, this time 4–0. Striker John Bosman scored five of Holland's eight goals in the first match but "only" a hat-trick in the replay.

England arrived in West Germany for the finals with the best record of any of the qualifiers, having won five and drawn one match, scoring 19 goals and conceding just one. But it appeared they had peaked too early and lost all three of their group matches. It started with a 1–0 setback against the Irish Republic newcomers and continuing with a devastating match against Holland, for whom Marco van Basten scored a hat-trick. The Soviet Union completed their misery, winning 3–1.

West Germany topped the other group then led Holland in their semi-final in Hamburg, thanks to a Lothar Matthaeus penalty after a foul on Jurgen Klinsmann. Holland hit back through a penalty of their own converted by Ronald Koeman, and Van Basten grabbed a late winner.

The other semi saw the Soviet Union maintain their fine record in the tournament with a 2–0 victory over Italy.

In the final, Holland met a Soviet side missing the significant defensive presence of Oleg Kuznetsov through suspension. Even Kuznetsov, however, would not have been able to control the attacking flair of Van Basten and skipper Ruud Gullit in the Dutch attack. Gullit scored the first goal and Van Basten the second – volleying home from Arnold Muhren's cross one of the greatest individual goals ever seen in any major international event.

The Soviet Union had a great chance to come back into the match when goalkeeper Hans van Breukelen carelessly conceded a penalty midway through the second half. But he redeemed himself by saving Igor Belanov's spot-kick, and Holland were rarely troubled thereafter.

Nobody could have foreseen that this would be the Soviet Union's swan-song in these championships.

Left: It's the goalkeeper's worst nightmare as Luis Arconada drops Platini's low drive and the ball spins agonisingly over the line **Right:** The future is orange: the Dutch triumverate of Van Aerle, Gullit and Van Basten after they go 2–0 in the 1988 final

DENMARK

"Denmark are a passionate football nation with a proud tradition. They won the European Championship in 1992 and the way they qualified for Euro 2004 shows their current team are very strong." England coach Sven-Goran Eriksson's assessment sums up Denmark's past and present.

Every Denmark side since 1992 is compared with the team of that year. They sprang the biggest shock in European Championship history when they beat Germany 2–0 in Gothenburg.

The current side qualified for Euro 2004 by topping Group Two. Qualification was fraught. They finished one point ahead of Norway and Romania, and two ahead of Bosnia-Herzegovina, after drawing 1–1 with the Bosnians in Sarajevo in their final qualifier. They held out for more than 50 minutes after Elvir Baljic equalised Martin Jorgensen's early goal.

Sixteen months earlier, Denmark had slid out of the World Cup, 3–0 to England in the last 16. Peter Schmeichel said at the time: "The Danish looked nervous and tense during the anthems, almost as though they were beaten before the start."

Coach Morten Olsen insisted it was different in Sarajevo. This time, Denmark showed their mental strength. He said: "It was a tough match but we played exactly as we'd planned – and we managed to resist the pressure from a fantastic crowd."

A month earlier, the Danes had shown more resilience to rescue a vital point against Romania, scoring late in a 2–2 draw. Later Bosnia won 2–0 in Copenhagen. Olsen held up his hands. He said: "I take responsibility. I picked the wrong team."

Denmark's English contingent launched their revival. Jesper Gronkjaer hit the only goal against Norway. Claus Jensen and then Thomas Gravesen scored in Luxembourg, to return Denmark to top spot before those last two games.

Now for Euro 2004. The Denmark coach is unlikely to gamble or experiment. He said: "We're looking to the players we know." His squad has a well-worn look. Most of the faces are familiar from the World Cup.

Their strength lies in attack. Olsen likes to play with width. PSV Eindhoven's Dennis Rommedahl and gifted but erratic Chelsea flier Gronkjaer can stretch the best defences.

Ebbe Sand has been a consistent scorer for Schalke in the Bundesliga. Jon Dahl Tomasson's goals helped win the 2002 UEFA Cup for Feyenoord and earned him a move to Milan. Their good days are thrilling – as when Rommedahl and Tomasson scored the time Denmark beat France 2–0 and confirmed the holders' early departure from the World Cup.

The midfield may lack the creativity to support them. They have no Beckham or Figo, let alone a Zidane or Vieira. Claus Jensen is their closest to a playmaker. Gravesen and Udinese's Martin Jorgensen supply more industry than subtlety. Inter's experienced Thomas Helveg is their only holding player. In defence, Milan's Martin Laursen is their cornerstone, supported by skipper and veteran Panathinaikos stopper Rene Henriksen. They still looked vulnerable to high balls in the qualifiers. Baljic's goal in Sarajevo was a header. So was John Carew's late equaliser for Norway in the 2–2 draw in Oslo. Olsen acknowledged: "We've had problems with long ball tactics like Norway use."

Denmark have the attackers to test the best. The question marks surround the men behind them. Goalkeeper Thomas Sorensen may be a busy man, but Olsen's teams usually guarantee action at both ends.

When the year ends in four, Denmark reach the European Championship semi-finals. So history says. In 1964, they lost 3–0 to the Soviet Union. In 1984, they lost on penalties to Spain after a 1–1 draw. After elimination at the group stages in Euro 2000 and Euro 96, the Danes would be delighted with such progress in Portugal.

Coach Morten Olsen

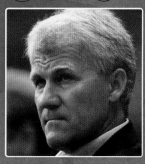

Olsen has rebuilt the team after an early exit from Euro 2000 when Bo Johansson's veterans failed to gain a point. Olsen employed a combination of experience and youth to steer Denmark to the 2002 World Cup finals and will repeat the formula for Euro 2004. Olsen was one of Denmark's greatest players, winning 102 caps in 19 years, including six seasons with Anderlecht and a spell with Koln in the Bundesliga. He coached Brondby, Koln and then Ajax before succeeding Johansson. Olsen is a forthright coach, who likes his players to show strong character and to attack with width. These have become the hallmarks of his Danish squad.

Championship Record

2000	–	1st rnd
1996	–	1st rnd
1992	–	champions
1988	–	1st rnd
1984	–	semi-finals
1980	–	did not qualify
1976	–	did not qualify
1972	–	did not qualify
1968	–	did not qualify
1964	–	semi-finals (4th)
1960	–	did not qualify

The Coach
Morten Olsen, aged 54
(born August 14, 1949)

Star Performers
Thomas Sorensen
Position: goalkeeper
Club: Aston Villa
Born: 12.6.1976

Rene Henriksen
Position: defender
Club: Panathinaikos
Born: 27.8.1969

Thomas Helveg
Position: defender/wing-back
Club: Internazionale
Born: 24.6.1971

Dennis Rommedahl
Position: winger
Club: PSV Eindhoven
Born: 22.7.1978

Ebbe Sand
Position: striker
Club: Schalke
Born: 19.7.1972

JON DAHL TOMASSON Aged 27 (born August 29, 1976). Striker Tomasson has found his greatest opportunity of attacking expression with Denmark since he has never been sure of a starting role with Milan in Italy's Serie A. The former Heerenveen, Feyenoord and Newcastle United forward was the Danes' five-goal top scorer in qualifying after making his debut in a 1–1 draw with Croatia back in 1997.

ITALY

Giovanni Trapattoni's original contract as national coach of Italy expires on June 30, three days before the European Championship Final in Lisbon. The odd timing was accidental and insignificant in its own way. If Italy get to the final, then Trapattoni expects to be at their head.

But, in another sense, the message is one of a new era of caution even though Italy will be among everyone else's favourites and boast a galaxy of attacking talent for which every other rival coach would give his eye teeth.

Trapattoni himself was an outstanding defensive wing-half in the 1960s and has always built his teams from the back. But even he came close to being swept away on a tide of negative hyperbole at the last World Cup when Italy, for all their talent, were shockingly beaten by co-hosts South Korea on a second-round golden goal. Part of the shock was in seeing a defence of high quality give away crucial goals with unexpected mistakes. One of the greatest surprises to emerge from the angry, embarrassed inquests which followed was that Trapattoni remained at his post. His use of substitutes was questioned along with his rotation tactic to try to accommodate all his star forwards at one time or another.

After Italy finished runners-up on a golden goal at Euro 2000, Trapattoni's predecessor Dino Zoff had quit in anger at one off-the-cuff remark from Milan owner and prime minister Silvio Berlusconi. Nothing Zoff had to endure was anything like as personal or critical as the attacks which rained down on Trapattoni. Yet, come the start of the following season, 'Trap' was still there.

The 2–1 Euro qualifying defeat by Wales in Cardiff prompted speculation about which successor would be in the job by the end of the year. But federation president Franco Carraro decided to stand by his man. The reward, for both veteran campaigners, was to see Italy turn their form and the group around then go top as the Welsh faded. Pippo Inzaghi's hat-trick to see off the Welsh finally in Milan was as much a personal victory for Trapattoni as it was excuse for national rejoicing. Everyone wanted to pull on the *Azzurri* shirt again. That victory settled Italy four points clear of Wales with just one defeat in their eight games,

a miserly goals conceded and 17 scored – the rate of just over two goals a game being a more than useful reference for an Italian team.

Milan's Inzaghi, with six goals, was Italy's leading scorer overall followed by Juventus' Alex Del Piero (five) and Inter's Christian Vieri (three). Boasting a depth of talent is no problem in any other sector of the team. Gianluigi Buffon and Francesco Toldo are two of the finest goalkeepers in the world, never mind Italy. Fabio Cannavaro and Alessandro Nesta have regained their old solidity in central defence after problems while they adjusted to new careers at Internazionale and Milan respectively. But the foundation for the qualifying revival was built on the hard-working contributions on the flanks of Mauro Camoranesi, Christian Panucci, Massimo Oddo and – above all – Gianluca Zambrotta. Their relentless support of midfield and attack has proved one of Italy's most effective weapons.

Italy play, at their most aggressive, with two strikers and one attacking midfielder. But with goal-grabbers Inzaghi and Vieri, support artists Del Piero and Francesco Totti plus Roma's fast-rising Antonio Cassano and Daniele De Rossi, picking the right combination from Italy's wealth of natural talent is a challenge. Trapattoni says of his team: "They have sacrificed their own natural game for the sake of the team. That's what football is about. It's a team game. It is when the individuals go their own way that problems start."

Trapattoni is determined that will not happen this year. Before the World Cup he said Italy's minimum aim was a place in the last four. He will not be the only Italian disappointed if that target is not fulfilled this time around.

Coach Giovanni Trapattoni

Trapattoni is the most successful coach among the entire managerial squad assembled for Euro 2004. However, his achievements in international and domestic cups and leagues were all in the club world with Milan, Juventus (twice), Inter, Bayern Munich (twice), Cagliari and Fiorentina. Brought up as a player with Milan in the *catenaccio* era, Trapattoni carried those safety-first values into his managerial career. He was in virtual semi-retirement when the Italian federation turned to him after Dino Zoff quit surprisingly following Euro 2000. Trapattoni's first test was the 2002 World Cup which ended in disaster, but somehow he survived to bring Italy back from the brink in Euro qualifying.

Championship Record

2000	–	runners-up
1996	–	1st rnd
1992	–	did not qualify
1988	–	semi-finals
1984	–	did not qualify
1980	–	semi-finals (H)
1976	–	did not qualify
1972	–	quarter-finals
1968	–	champions (H)
1964	–	did not qualify
1960	–	did not enter

The Coach

Giovanni Trapattoni, aged 65
(born March 17, 1939)

Star Performers

Gianluigi Buffon
Position: goalkeeper
Club: Juventus
Born: 28.1.1978

Alessandro Nesta
Position: defender
Club: Milan
Born: 19.3.1976

Alessandro 'Alex' Del Piero
Position: midfield/forward
Club: Juventus
Born: 9.11.1974

Christian Vieri
Position: forward
Club: Internazionale
Born: 12.7.1973

Filippo 'Pippo' Inzaghi
Position: forward
Club: Milan
Born: 9.8.1973

FRANCESCO TOTTI Aged 27 (born September 27, 1976). Roma skipper Totti has been one of the outstanding personalities in Serie A ever since making his Italy debut in a 2–0 win over Switzerland in Udinese on October 10, 1998. Has remained an Italy squad regular despite competition from the likes of Alessandro Del Piero. Briefly blotted his record when he was sent off in the World Cup upset by South Korea.

SWEDEN

In recent years, Sweden have been good enough to compete with the best, but never quite good enough to beat them. Now they must go into battle against Europe's finest without their biggest threat, the Celtic goal machine Henrik Larsson who has retired from the international game.

Coaching duo Tommy Soderberg and Lars Lagerback have taken the Swedes to Euro 2000 and the 2002 World Cup finals. They were eliminated from Euro 2000 after the first group stage.

They topped their World Cup 'group of death' – which included England, Argentina and Nigeria – then lost to Senegal in the last 16. The Swedes were knocked out by Henri Camara's 'golden goal' after a 1–1 draw at 90 minutes. Larsson had headed them into an 11th-minute lead.

That was one of 24 goals the Celtic striker scored in 72 games for his country. Larsson, 32, quit after Sweden's 2–0 qualifying win over Hungary in April 2003, to concentrate on club football. Aston Villa striker Marcus Allback has accepted the role of Larsson's successor. He scored both goals against Hungary in Budapest. He also missed an 87th-minute penalty in Sweden's 1–0 home defeat by Latvia, although qualification was already assured.

But Allback has struggled for goals in the Premiership and Sweden's most potent efforts are likely to come from two other players – Zlatan Ibrahimovic and Freddie Ljungberg.

Ibrahimovic, 22, is the maverick of the squad. The former Malmo striker offers pace, invention and finishing power. He has been one of Ajax's most impressive performers in the Champions League and he scored three goals for Sweden in the qualifiers. He can be inspirational – or peripheral. As he says: "My moves just come to me. They're nothing that I plan."

Ljungberg is battle-hardened with Arsenal. They use him as a wide midfielder who drifts into scoring positions. He plays a more central role for Sweden, dribbling at pace behind the front two or working as a support striker. He has an extra incentive to excel at Euro 2004, after a hip injury wrecked his World Cup campaign when he was in top form.

On the wings are Brondby's Mattias Jonson, who scored a hat-trick against San Marino in the qualifiers, and Malmo's Niklas Skoog, the Swedish league top scorer.

Skoog is one of the young players – along with goalkeeper Andreas Isaksson and midfielder Mikael Nilsson – who came through the Sweden team that won the King's Cup in Thailand last year. Thailand's then coach, Englishman Peter Withe, said: "They play physical football and they're tactically shrewd." The Swedes make good use of those physical qualities at dead ball moves, when centre-backs Michael Svensson and Olof Mellberg trot forward.

When Sweden lost 1–0 to the Latvians last year, it ended a run of 25 games unbeaten at home, stretching back to 1997. Soderberg was philosophical. He said: "I think the players have shown that they're at their best on the big occasions."

He will hope that proves true in Portugal. But he and Lagerback know that Sweden's central defence can be turned by quick attackers. Their midfield lacks subtlety too. The likes of Tobias Linderoth and Pontus Farnerud will run forever, but the creative force rests all too heavily on Anders Svensson.

Sweden made their best Euro-showing on home ground in 1992. A team including Tomas Brolin, Martin Dahlin and Stefan Schwarz reached the semi-finals. They lost 3–2 to Germany. Thomas Hassler and Karl-Heinz Riedle put the Germans 2–0 up after 58 minutes. Brolin replied. Riedle added Germany's third. Kennet Andersson's goal came too late.

The Swedes have reached the last eight on one other occasion. They were disappointed to lose 4–2 on aggregate to the Soviet Union in 1964. But a quarter-final finish this time would probably delight the nation.

Coach Tommy Soderberg & Lars Lagerback

Tommy Soderberg hopes to exit with a flourish at Euro 2004 after deciding to step aside after the finals. He has been in charge since 1997 and was joined a year later by Lars Lagerback, who has shared responsibility. Soderberg says: "If we'd failed to qualify, I'd have gone in October. Now the dream is to round it all off in Portugal." Soderberg and Lagerback also guided Sweden to the finals of Euro 2000 and the last 16 at the 2002 World Cup finals. Soderberg steered AIK Stockholm to the 1992 league title. Lagerback has worked for the Swedish federation since 1990.

Championship Record

2000	–	1st rnd
1996	–	did not qualify
1992	–	semi-finals (H)
1988	–	did not qualify
1984	–	did not qualify
1980	–	did not qualify
1976	–	did not qualify
1972	–	did not qualify
1968	–	did not qualify
1964	–	quarter-finals
1960	–	did not enter

The Coach

Tommy Soderberg, aged 55
(born August 19, 1948)

Star Performers

Andreas Isaksson
Position: goalkeeper
Club: Djurgardens
Born: 3.10.1981

Johan Mjallby
Position: defender
Club: Celtic
Born: 9.2.1971

Teddy Lucic
Position: defender
Club: Bayer Leverkusen
Born: 15.4.1973

Marcus Allback
Position: forward
Club: Aston Villa
Born: 5.7.1973

Zlatan Ibrahimovic
Position: forward
Club: Ajax
Born: 3.10.1981

OLOF MELLBERG Aged 26 (born September 3, 1977). Central defender Mellberg has been one of the cornerstones of the Swedish national team since making his debut in a 1–0 defeat by Italy in Palermo in February 2000. He had already moved abroad then with Santander, switching to the Premiership with Aston Villa for £5million in 2001. He was one of Sweden's ever-presents at the last World Cup finals.

BULGARIA

The best of Bulgaria is still to come, according to coach Plamen Markov who will take one of the youngest of the 16 squads to the finals. Reaching the European finals is only the start for the former international midfielder who is hoping to repeat the heroics of Bulgaria's last big tournament.

Bulgaria have not appeared in a major finals since they finished a remarkable but well-deserved fourth at the World Cup in the United States in 1994. Markov was a member of the midfield engine room in that team which was sparked to a place among the elite by the creative talents of Hristo Stoichkov, Emil Kostadinov and Yordan Lechkov.

They were the first talented players to be permitted by the then communist authorities to transfer out of Bulgarian football and sharpen their talents in Spain and Germany. They took their new-found technical and tactical expertise back home to raise the standard and status of the national team. Now Markov has further profited from that freedom to guide Bulgaria to the promise of new adventures as coach. Even the tempestuous Stoichkov, who scored six goals in the 1994 World Cup, has only praise for Markov's men, saying: "What they have achieved is fantastic for Bulgarian football. They have enormous promise and great team spirit and they can play together for years to come. That means exciting times ahead for our fans."

Markov has not had it easy. Veteran playmaker Krasimir Balakov retired from all football in the middle of the qualifying campaign, defender Radostin Kishishev retired from the national team, then the attack was weakened by a long-term injury to Portsmouth striker Svetoslav Todorov. But Bulgaria retain an iron backbone through the likes of Zdravko Zdravkov in goal, Daniel Birimirov at wing-back, Stilian Petrov in midfield, Stuttgart's Martin Petrov on the wing and Dimitar Berbatov up front.

Bulgaria won qualifying Group Eight in style with a game to spare after five wins from their first seven matches. The fact they lost their concluding match 1–0 in Croatia was a mere blip on Markov's radar screen.

The decisive match for Bulgaria was a comfortable 3–0 qualifying win over Andorra in September. Markov and his men then locked themselves away in their hotel to watch TV coverage of the match between Belgium and Croatia. The Belgians' win meant Bulgaria could celebrate their place in the finals with a game to spare - and Markov could enjoy the mother of all parties to celebrate his 46th birthday the following day.

Markov picked up the reins after Stoicho Mladenov's exit following a 6–0 thrashing by the Czech Republic in the World Cup qualifiers in October 2001. He was not the obvious choice. Spells in charge of his old club CSKA Sofia and home-town Vidima-Rakovksi hardly ranked as a high-quality CV.

But he has done all the necessary homework. Markov says: "I studied the results and methods of the best coaches in Europe and adapted those ideas which could best suit my personal vision and way of working. Sometimes I wish I could put my boots back on again and get out on the pitch when things are going badly but my career is over. A coach's contribution is before kick-off. For us, the match finishes before it starts."

Less than half of the current national squad play for Bulgarian clubs which means Markov's time with his players is limited. The majority are spread far and wide across Europe. Like a number of Euro finalists, however, Bulgaria will worry about the goal supply. They scored an economic 13 in their eight qualifying ties and only Bayer Leverkusen's Berbatov has topped double figures in international football. For all the burgeoning new talent, there is no new Stoichkov or Kostadinov on the horizon.

Not that Markov will let that affect his optimism. He says: "I never doubted my mission would come to a perfect end. The lads also believed in me. But we still have a lot of work to do. The real job starts now."

Coach Plamen Markov

Markov took over as national coach from former international team-mate Stoicho Mladenov in December 2001 after Bulgaria's failure to qualify for the World Cup. He was a surprise choice after modest spells in charge of Rakovski, CSKA Sofia, Metz and Grenoble. But his studious approach and motivational talents quickly revived confidence and morale. Markov had scored six goals in 38 appearances in midfield for Bulgaria in the 1980s. He won a string of domestic leagues and cups with army team CSKA before becoming one of Bulgaria's first footballing exports when he took up a contract in France with Metz as a gesture of thanks for his services.

Championship Record

2000	– did not qualify
1996	– 1st rnd
1992	– did not qualify
1988	– did not qualify
1984	– did not qualify
1980	– did not qualify
1976	– did not qualify
1972	– did not qualify
1968	– quarter-finals
1964	– did not qualify
1960	– did not qualify

The Coach
Plamen Markov, aged 46
(born September 11, 1957)

Star Performers
Zdravko Zdravkov
Position: goalkeeper
Club: Istanbulspor
Born: 4.10.1970

Daniel Borimirov
Position: wing-back/midfield
Club: TSV 1860 Munich
Born: 15.1.1970

Stilian Petrov
Position: midfield
Club: Celtic
Born: 5.7.1979

Marian Hristov
Position: midfield
Club: Kaiserslautern
Born: 29.7.1973

Martin Petrov
Position: winger
Club: Wolfsburg
Born: 15.1.1979

DIMITAR BERBATOV Aged 23 (born January 30, 1981). Rangy forward Berbatov is a leader of the new generation of Bulgarian stars. The former CSKA Sofia striker has been a key man in the rise of Germany's Bayer Leverkusen with whom he was a Champions League runner-up in 2000. Berbatov made his Bulgaria debut in a 1–0 loss to Greece in 1999 and was Bulgaria's five-goal top scorer in the Euro qualifiers.

GREAT MOMENTS FROM THE PAST

Defying all the odds, Denmark are called back from the beach to take the place of Yugoslavia and come racing in from the football wilderness with explosive results against the giants of both Holland and Germany in Sweden... but, four years later, the Germans take their revenge in more ways than one as England play host to the European Championship but bow out in an emotional semi-final against their great rivals.

Denmark sprang the greatest surprise in European Championship history when their 'Danish Dynamite' exploded underneath the 1992 finals in Sweden.

Remarkably, the Danes had not originally reached the tournament after finishing runners-up to Yugoslavia in qualifying. Manager Richard Moller Nielsen was at home decorating his kitchen when he was asked to recall his players from their holidays.

The entire event had been subject to political upheavals, with former East Germany consigned to history just as qualifying began and the Soviet Union transformed, briefly, into the Commonwealth of Independent States.

But the greatest complication was prompted by the violent collapse of Yugoslavia in the spring of 1992 after the death of Tito exposed fissures in the structure of the republic. UEFA barred them from the finals on security grounds and sent for Denmark at two weeks' notice.

The Swedish hosts, in the finals for the first time, deservedly topped group A. Tomas Brolin's wonderful goal brought them a 2–1 victory over a disappointing England on the last matchday.

Denmark were runners-up in the group, thanks to a 2–1 victory over an under-achieving French side managed by their old hero Platini (he would quit after their first-round failure and later take on the co-presidency of the French organising committee for the 1998 World Cup finals).

In Group B, Holland and Germany possessed too much firepower and experience for newcomers Scotland and the CIS, although Germany did need a last-minute goal from Thomas Hassler to snatch a point from their opening game against the CIS.

Left: Goalie's ball: Peter Schmeichel gets to a cross before Jurgen Klinsmann as the Danes pull off one of the greatest-ever surprises in world football **Right:** Klinsmann has the last laugh as Germany beat the Czech Republic in the 1996 final

The two semi-finals produced great entertainment. Holland – imperious in qualifying – threw theirs away against Denmark, being held 2–2 and losing 5–4 on penalties. Remarkably the decisive penalty miss was contributed by Marco van Basten, the hero four years earlier. Brolin scored again for Sweden in the other semi-final, but this time in vain in a 3–2 defeat by Germany.

Berti Vogts's men were clear favourites in the final. But Denmark – from manager Moller Nielsen through goalkeeper Peter Schmeichel, skipper Lars Olsen, midfielder Kim Vilfort and forward Brian Laudrup – had not read the script. Goals from John Jensen and Vilfort – allied to the rock-solid inspiration of 'Great Dane' Schmeichel and sweeper Olsen – had duly produced one of the greatest shocks in the competition's history.

UEFA enlarged the tournament again from eight to 16 teams for England's staging in 1996. The hosts drew 1–1 against Switzerland in their opener before pulling themselves together with a dramatic 2–0 victory over old enemy Scotland and a high-class 4–1 defeat of Holland.

France topped Group B ahead of Spain, while the confrontation of eastern European pride and western European fantasy was repeated in Group D, where holders Denmark were dethroned by Croatia and the Portuguese. Italy were notable failures in Group C from which both the Germans and Czechs qualified.

The quality of football faded in the knock-out stages in which spot-kicks proved decisive for both England (against Spain) and France (against Holland). The Czechs surprisingly beat Portugal 1–0 while Germany triumphed 2–1 in a bad-tempered duel with Croatia.

Penalties were needed to resolve both the semi-finals, with the Czechs pipping France after a dull 0–0 draw at Old Trafford. However England v Germany provided a night of exciting intensity which a 76,000 crowd at Wembley and 26million domestic television viewers will never forget.

England secured a magnificent start, Alan Shearer heading home in the third minute but the Germans soon levelled through their only fit striker, Stefan Kuntz. The drama rolled on into golden-goal extra-time when Darren Anderton struck a post and Kuntz had a headed effort disallowed.

Both sides converted their five spotkicks but Gareth Southgate, by pushing the next kick into the arms of keeper Andy Kopke, offered Andy Moller the chance to shoot Germany into the final.

Domestic euphoria might have been punctured like a toy balloon. Yet it said everything for the manner in which Euro 96 had gripped the public imagination that 73,611 turned out for the final at Wembley. The vast majority – English fans converted into honorary Czechs for the night – were celebrating when Patrick Berger fired home a 59th-minute penalty.

Germany had lost to underdogs in the final – against Denmark – four years earlier in Sweden and history appeared about to repeat itself. Then German coach Berti Vogts played his hidden ace, bringing on substitute centre-forward Oliver Bierhoff. Within four minutes Bierhoff had headed the Germans level then, in the fourth minute of extra time, he fired home the golden goal.

The Czechs protested that Kuntz had been standing in an offside position, but Italian referee Pierluigi Pairetto waved away their protests. An Italian linesman had proved a winner for Germany in the stadium where an Azerbaijani linesman had proved a loser in the World Cup 30 years earlier.

Unlike that World Cup, the hosts had not lifted the trophy. But they won just about everything else. Outgoing coach Terry Venables' last duty was to accept the UEFA Fairplay trophy and centre-forward Alan Shearer was crowned the tournament's five-goal top scorer.

GERMANY

Germany left it late, but, as usual, they took up their invitation to the party in Portugal. Yet the enigma of Germany's national team remains. More than a decade has passed since the former triple European champions put together a team and a run of form which impressed the watching world.

And yet – here they are again. Ever since, as West Germany, first entering the then Nations Cup in 1968, they have failed only once to reach at least the quarter-finals. Two years ago, to their own surprise, they found themselves in the World Cup Final in Yokohama. They lost 2–0 to Brazil, but their very presence extended the intimidatory legend that German teams never know when they are beaten.

Their progress to Portugal further illustrated the point. The Germans lost away to the minnows of Iceland, feared the possibility of a play-off against Holland or Spain, then secured top place in the group by turning over the Icelanders in their last match back in Hamburg.

Intriguingly, Voller lined up only three of the men who started the World Cup Final against Iceland: goalkeeper-captain Oliver Kahn, defensive midfielder Carsten Ramelow and midfield workhorse Bernd Schneider. Injuries had taken their toll on the likes of Christoph Metzelder and Christian Ziege, midfielder Dietmar Hamann and winger Sebastian Deisler.

But in football one player's injury is another player's opportunity.

Almost without anyone noticing, Voller has begun to draw on a new seam of youngsters whose promise may be fulfilled not in Portugal but – more importantly to German fans – when they host the World Cup in two years' time. Two of those newcomers are from reviving Stuttgart: defender Andreas Hinkel and Brazil-born striker Kevin Kuranyi.

In tactical terms the Germans remain as predictable and true to their Bundesliga roots as ever. Voller, who picked up the managerial reins in emergency in 2000 after a drugs scandal enveloped Christoph Daum, relies on the aggressive goalkeeping of Kahn to command the three-man back line ahead of him.

Hertha Berlin's Arne Friedrich has emerged on the right with Leverkusen's reliable Ramelow in the middle and Borussia Dortmund's Christian Worns on the left. The engine room is a five-man midfield whose work ethic is enlivened by the talent of the one German player who, for sheer talent, stands head and shoulders above his team-mates: Michael Ballack.

Ballack emerged on the international stage in the spring of 2002. He led Bayer Leverkusen to the Champions League Final (where they lost to Real Madrid) and then guided Germany to the World Cup Final. His self-sacrificing spirit also cost him his place in that final; Ballack committed a foul in the semi-final which earned a yellow card and suspension.

Already he had agreed to join Bayern Munich and he was their league and cup double-winning inspiration in 2003. The Midas touch spilled over for Germany: Ballack struck the nerve-settling ninth-minute goal in the decisive 3–0 win over Iceland. The strike left him as the Germans' joint qualifying top marksman on four goals with Fredi Bobic. Up front the striking duo is made up by a permutation of the 'old boy' Bobic along with new boy Kuranyi and Miroslav Klose. Voller was more relieved than anything when Ballack, Bobic and Kuranyi won the day against Iceland, saying: "Reaching the finals is a great achievement considering all our injuries. We have had to rebuild almost the entire team since the World Cup and that is a dangerous job to undertake during a qualifying competition. I can only say that my players responded magnificently."

But Voller never sets his targets too high. He has tipped France, Italy and Portugal as Euro finals favourites. As for Germany: "We just want to get through the first round. That's the basic aim." But then, he said that before the 2002 World Cup as well.

Coach Rudi Voller

Voller has had one of the most testing reigns of any German coach with serious concerns about a dearth of youthful talent. Voller was centre-forward when Germany won the World Cup in 1990 and enjoyed an outstanding club career with Werder Bremen and Roma. He later became general manager at Leverkusen who loaned him to the federation as caretaker manager in 2000–01. He stayed on full time after a drugs scandal ruled out nominated successor Christoph Daum. Reaching the 2002 World Cup Final was a huge achievement against all odds and expectations.

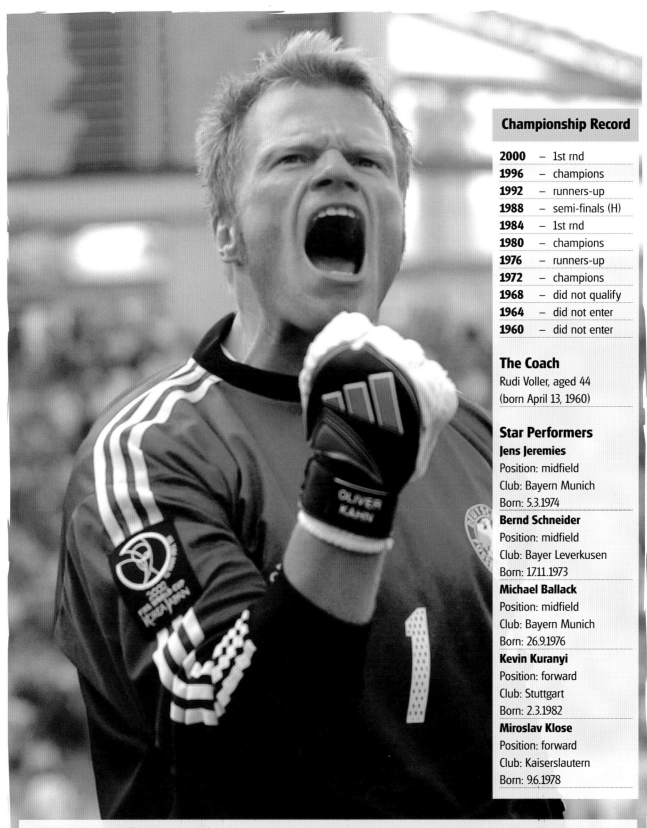

Championship Record

2000	–	1st rnd
1996	–	champions
1992	–	runners-up
1988	–	semi-finals (H)
1984	–	1st rnd
1980	–	champions
1976	–	runners-up
1972	–	champions
1968	–	did not qualify
1964	–	did not enter
1960	–	did not enter

The Coach
Rudi Voller, aged 44
(born April 13, 1960)

Star Performers
Jens Jeremies
Position: midfield
Club: Bayern Munich
Born: 5.3.1974

Bernd Schneider
Position: midfield
Club: Bayer Leverkusen
Born: 17.11.1973

Michael Ballack
Position: midfield
Club: Bayern Munich
Born: 26.9.1976

Kevin Kuranyi
Position: forward
Club: Stuttgart
Born: 2.3.1982

Miroslav Klose
Position: forward
Club: Kaiserslautern
Born: 9.6.1978

OLIVER KAHN Aged 34 (born June 15, 1969). Kahn has emerged as the aggressively consistent goalkeeper-captain of both Germany and Bayern Munich over the past three years. Son of an old Bundesliga pro, he began with Karlsruhe, then, with Bayern, won all the top European and domestic prizes. Kahn, voted top player at the 2002 World Cup, made his Germany debut in a 2–1 win over Switzerland in Bern in June 1995.

HOLLAND

Holland are the great under-achievers of international football. Since winning the 1988 European Championship, they have failed again and again to fulfil their potential. This time the Dutch are out to show the world what Total Football means and they have the players to succeed.

The Dutch produce a seemingly endless production line of class players. But they squander their talent through in-fighting off the field. No wonder coach Dick Advocaat greeted qualification by saying: "We have enormous quality but it's high time for achievement."

In Sweden during Euro 92 the Dutch were so focused on meeting old rivals Germany in the final that they underestimated Denmark and lost the semi-final 5–4 on penalties after a 2–2 draw. Peter Schmeichel saved the crucial kick from Marco Van Basten, one of Holland's all-time heroes.

At Euro 96 in England the squad squabbled amid reports of racial tension. At home as co-hosts for Euro 2000, the Dutch subsided in the semi-final against Italy. They lost another shoot-out, against a side reduced to 10 men after Zambrotta's expulsion. Holland wasted two penalty chances to take victory. In between the misfiring Euro shoot-outs, Holland had lost another penalty contest to Brazil in the 1998 World Cup semi-finals in France. Dennis Bergkamp, a veteran of all four defeats, said: "I don't know why we can't win a shoot-out. It's stupid. It goes back to 1992 against Denmark. With the players we've had over the years, we should have achieved more. But we're not like other teams. As a nation, we're strong-minded and everyone has his own opinion. Everyone wants to say something and that can create disharmony."

Indiscipline was a problem again in the Euro 2004 qualifiers. The Dutch lost the decisive Group Three clash against the Czech Republic 3–1 after playing for 76 minutes with 10 men. Ruud Van Nistelrooy was then suspended by the Dutch federation, the KNVB, after he reacted furiously to being substituted 20 minutes from time – kicking over a water bottle and screaming at the bench.

Ultimately, Holland reached the finals by a typically circuitous route. They finished second in the group with 19 points, more than seven of the other nine group winners. They then lost the play-off first leg, 1–0 against Scotland in Glasgow, before strolling through the return 6–0 when Van Nistelrooy scored a hat-trick. Holland's performance in Glasgow infuriated the nation and led to calls for Advocaat's resignation yet, four days later, they cut the Scots to ribbons. It was soccer schizophrenia.

The talent at Advocaat's disposal glitters. Vastly experienced defenders Frank De Boer, Michael Reiziger and Jaap Stam protect Holland's most-capped keeper, Edwin Van der Sar. Holland's boss can perm from a formidable mixture of midfield experience and youthful exuberance. Philip Cocu, Edgar Davids, Mark Van Bommel and Clarence Seedorf are tried and tested. So are Marc Overmars and Bodo Zenden on the flanks. Ajax skipper Rafael Van der Vaart leads the younger generation, backed by the promising Wesley Sneijder and Inter winger Andy van der Meyde. All three started against the Scots in Amsterdam – a clear hint that Advocaat is likely to rebalance an ageing team with an injection of youth at the finals in Portugal.

In attack it's Holland's record scorer Patrick Kluivert, Roy Makaay, Jimmy Floyd Hasselbaink and Ruud Van Nistelrooy. The Mancheser United man has a point to prove in his first major finals after missing Euro 2000 through injury. He says: "It's vital for me and the rest of the players to do well at Euro 2004 because we want to show how good Dutch football is."

Midfielder Gio Van Bronckhorst summed it up: "Everyone sees Euro 2004 as an opportunity to put the record straight and prove that the last World Cup was an isolated mistake. We have the names in our team. All we need now are the results to match."

Coach Dick Advocaat

Advocaat is in his second spell as Holland coach. He was assistant to the great Rinus Michels between 1984 and 1987, before he took his first major club job with Haarlem. Advocaat was appointed boss for the first time in 1992 after steering SVV Dordrecht into Holland's top division. He stamped his authority by dismissing Ruud Gullit from the squad after a half-time row. Then he led the Dutch to the quarter-finals of the 1994 World Cup. Returning to club football with PSV Eindhoven, Advocaat then succeeded Walter Smith at Rangers in 1998. He rejoined the Dutch set-up after Louis van Gaal's 2002 resignation, initially as part-time boss then full-time.

Championship Record

2000	–	semi-finals
1996	–	quarter-finals
1992	–	semi-finals
1988	–	champions
1984	–	did not qualify
1980	–	1st rnd
1976	–	third place
1972	–	did not qualify
1968	–	did not qualify
1964	–	did not qualify
1960	–	did not enter

The Coach

Dick Advocaat, aged 56
(born September 27, 1947)

Star Performers

Edwin Van der Sar
Position: goalkeeper
Club: Fulham
Born: 19.10.1970

Frank De Boer
Position: defender
Club: Galatasaray
Born: 15.5.1970

Edgar Davids
Position: midfield
Club: Juventus
Born: 13.3.1973

Rafael Van der Vaart
Position: forward
Club: Ajax Amsterdam
Born: 11.2.1983

Patrick Kluivert
Position: forward
Club: Barcelona
Born: 1.7.1976

RUUD VAN NISTELROOY Aged 27 (born July 1, 1976). Van Nistelrooy has managed an amazing comeback after a career-threatening knee injury to establish himself as one of Europe's most dangerous strikers. The injury cost him a place in Holland's Euro 2000 squad but he has since been busy making up for lost time. The £19million which Manchester United paid PSV Eindhoven in 2001 now looks a steal.

CZECH REPUBLIC

Karel Bruckner's rejuvenated Czech Republic squad were among the most impressive qualifiers for Euro 2004. They topped Group Three with seven wins and a draw – a crucial 1–1 scoreline away to Holland. They clinched their place with a game to spare after a win over the mighty Dutch.

The 3–2 victory over Austria which followed was their 18th successive game unbeaten under Bruckner, who was promoted from the Under-21 squad after the Czechs flopped against Belgium in the 2002 World Cup play-offs. Bruckner has brought discipline to the squad and injected youth too, by promoting the best of the 'zlate generace' (golden generation) – the players who won the European Under-21 championship in 2002.

The Czechs' World Cup campaign was dogged by indiscipline. Defender Tomas Repka was sent off in the first match; Pavel Nedved and Milan Baros saw red in the second. Repka had also missed Euro 96 in England because of a sending-off before the tournament. So when Repka said he did not want to play for the national side, Bruckner let him walk into international oblivion. It was a symbolic moment. Critics had accused previous coach Jozef Chovanec of being too lax with the players. They would not level that accusation against Bruckner.

The new coach believes in young talent. He put his faith in Under-21 keeper Petr Cech and full-back Zdenek Gygera. He gave regular outings to Under-21 striker Milan Baros and called up young defender Tomas Hubschman. He made Hamburg's Tomas Ujfalusi the cornerstone of his back line, then installed experienced centre-back Rene Bolf to partner him.

Bruckner blended them with the big names: dashing skipper Nedved, evergreen Karel Poborsky, young playmaker Tomas Rosicky and giant striker Jan Koller. The Czechs' unbeaten run throughout 2002 restored morale and team spirit.

When the Czechs beat France 2–0 in Paris in a friendly in February last year, home coach Jacques Santini said: "We couldn't match their appetite."

A month later Bruckner's team drew 1–1 in Holland when Koller tucked away Baros's flick to equalise Ruud Van Nistelrooy's goal. It was a crucial moment. The Czechs clinched their place in Portugal with two wins in four September days.

Then, in Prague, Poborsky ran the show as the Czechs beat Holland 3–1. Koller netted a penalty after Edgar Davids was sent off for a second yellow card. Poborsky added the second. Rafael van der Vaart replied with a deflected shot. The Czechs kept their discipline. Baros rounded Edwin van der Sar to score their third in stoppage time. Bruckner said: "It was unbelievable how much energy Poborsky showed."

The coach says that Euro 2004 places are up for grabs until the last moment. But he knows his main men. The doubt is Baros, who suffered a broken ankle playing for Liverpool at Blackburn, three days after the Holland game. If he fails to recover, Bruckner will look to the formation which started against the Dutch in Prague – Koller as a lone striker, Nedved, Poborsky and Smicer in support and Rosicky pulling the strings.

The Czechs have a proud history in the European Championship. They won the competition in 1976 as Czechoslovakia, thanks to Antonin Panenka's famous shoot-out penalty against Germany. As the Czech Republic, they lost the Euro 96 final to Germany.

Four years later, the Czechs were eliminated from the 'group of death' at Euro 2000, when Youri Djorkaeff's goal earned France the 2–1 win that sent the Czechs home. Nedved remembers all too well. He says: "We have a really strong group of players right now. We've had the benefit of playing for some of the biggest clubs in Europe. Now I want to leave behind a legacy that other people will admire."

It may be a long time before the Czechs have a better chance.

Coach Karel Bruckner

Bruckner has revitalised the Czech squad after their failure to reach the 2002 World Cup. He succeeded Jozef Chovanec after guiding the Czech Under-21s and Under-23s to the 2000 Sydney Olympics. He also led them to the European Under-21 final in 2000 and a 3–1 shoot-out win over France in the 2002 European final. With the senior side, he cleared out the ageing stars from Euro 2000 to make way for his junior protégés, including Petr Cech, Zdenek Grygera and Milan Baros. At club level Bruckner bossed Inter Bratislava, Sigma Olomouc and Drnovice. He sums up his approach by saying: "A sense of responsibility is critical in a job like this."

Championship Record

2000	–	1st rnd
1996	–	runners-up
1992	–	did not qualify
As Czechoslovakia:		
1988	–	did not qualify
1984	–	did not qualify
1980	–	third place
1976	–	champions
1972	–	did not qualify
1968	–	did not qualify
1964	–	did not qualify
1960	–	semi-finals (3rd)

The Coach

Karel Bruckner, aged 64
(born March 4, 1940)

Star Performers

Petr Cech
Position: goalkeeper
Club: Rennes
Born: 20.5.1982

Zdenek Grygera
Position: defender
Club: Ajax
Born: 14.5.1980

Vladimir Smicer
Position: midfield
Club: Liverpool
Born: 24.5.1973

Karel Poborsky
Position: forward
Club: Sparta Prague
Born: 30.3.1972

Jon Koller
Position: forward
Club: Borussia Dortmund
Born: 30.3.1973

PAVEL NEDVED Aged 31 (born August 30, 1982). Playmaker Nedved is the finest player to emerge since the Czech Republic split with Slovakia at the start of the 1990s. His achievements in Italy with Lazio and Juventus have been matched by his inspirational leadership of his country. Several times domestic Footballer of the Year, Nedved made his Czech debut in a 3–1 win in the Irish Republic in June 1994.

LATVIA

Latvia fans will never forget how their rank outsiders achieved the greatest shock in the Euro 2004 qualifiers by reaching the finals in Portugal. But can the Baltic nation's counter-attacking style keep coming up trumps when they have to take on the big boys of European football?

On November 18, the Latvian people partied to mark the 12th anniversary of their independence from the old Soviet Union. A day later, they took to the streets after Aleksandrs Starkovs's squad came from 2–0 down in Turkey to reach the nation's first major finals.

They did it the hard way. First they ended Group Four winners Sweden's 25-game unbeaten home record 1–0 in their concluding qualifying tie. That set up a play-off against Turkey, the 2002 World Cup semi-finalists.

Maris Verpakovskis scored the only goal on a freezing day in Riga, when Latvia came through injuries, suspensions, persistent Turkish pressure as well as altercations in the players' tunnel. Defenders Mihails Zemlinskis and Dzintars Zirnis returned from bans for the second leg in Istanbul. But Latvia were staring at elimination when Hakan Sukur scored Turkey's second goal after 64 minutes. That was before Footballer of the Year Jurijs Laizans deceived keeper Omer Catkic with a swinging free-kick and the prolific Verpakovskis lobbed the second with 12 minutes left.

It was a defining moment for the Baltic nation of 2.3 million. Crowds poured onto the streets of the capital, Riga. Coach Starkovs and his squad were mobbed at the airport. Starkovs was feted like a conquering general for his counter-attacking tactics. He said: "It's a historic success for our country and it's caused a sensation across Europe. I can hardly believe it and I'm not sure how to react. The players have raised our targets so high."

Football has historically vied with ice hockey as Latvia's favourite sport. Suddenly football reigns but Portugal in 2004 will be the hard part for Starkovs's squad who will need every inspirational gem Laizans can dig up.

The 25-year-old midfielder toppled the Turks weeks after helping inspire CSKA Moscow's Russian championship victory with spectacular goals – similar to the one with which Latvia beat Poland in Warsaw along the Euro qualifying way. But if Latvia are to prosper, he needs to control the temper which earned a red card for an off-the-ball lunge at Mariusz Lewandowski when Poland won in Riga.

Verpakovskis is a rising star. The Skonto Riga striker has scored five goals in his last four competitive games for Latvia. He has grown in confidence in the absence of the once-talismanic Marian Pahars, sidelined for more than a year with ankle injuries. His partnership with the nippy Ventspils attacker Vits Rimkus will test the pace of the best defences.

Latvia attack on the break. It's no coincidence that they have gained their best wins away. Starkovs bases tactics on an experienced back line in front of keeper Alex Kolinko. His side conceded only eight goals in eight group matches and two play-offs. Everyone tracks back, even the strikers.

English fans will recognise several names. Beveren centre-back Igors Stepanvos played for Arsenal, and Kolinko and Andrejs Rubins both turned out for Crystal Palace, while Vitalijs Astafjevs, now with Austrian club Admira, played for Bristol Rovers. Somehow when they play for Starkovs their whole seems greater than the sum of their parts.

The Latvia coach is a shrewd organiser with tactical nous, as he proved in the play-offs. He said: "We work long and hard at these things. We studied Turkey well. They didn't surprise us. We play intelligent football and we got our tactics right. It suits us to play on the counter-attack because we have quick and technically gifted players."

Desire may not be enough in the finals. But Starkovs and his squad enter Euro 2004 unburdened by the weight of expectation. He said: "I'm happy that we're portrayed as underdogs. That has suited us well so far."

Coach Aleksandrs Starkovs

Starkovs has flown the flag for Latvia as both player and coach. First Starkovs was the foremost domestic striker of his generation with Daugava, top Latvian team of the Soviet era. He finished as Soviet second division top-scorer during their 1977 promotion bid, form that earned him a move to Dynamo Moscow. He spent one season in the Russian capital before returning to Riga. He played 301 games for Daugava. Starkovs began coaching as an assistant at Daugava, then steered Skonto Riga to nine consecutive domestic titles. He was aide to national coaches Revaz Dzodzashvili and Gary Johnson before succeeding Johnson in May 2001.

Championship Record

2000 – did not qualify
1996 – did not qualify
1960-92 – did not exist

The Coach
Aleksandrs Starkovs,
aged 48 (born July 26, 1955)

Star Performers
Alex Kolinko
Position: goalkeeper
Club: Rostselmash Rostov
Born: 18.6.1975

Mikhails Zemlinskis
Position: defender
Club: Skonto Riga
Born: 21.12.1969

Vitalijs Astafjevs
Position: midfield
Club: Admira Wacker
Born: 3.4.1971

Maris Verpakovskis
Position: forward
Club: Skonto Riga
Born: 15.10.1979

Marian Pahars
Position: striker
Club: Southampton
Born: 5.8.1976

JURIJS LAIZANS Aged 25 (born January 6, 1979). Laizans took over from Marian Pahars as Latvia's talisman in 2002 when he was voted Footballer of the Year in recognition of his success with Russian club CSKA Moscow. Laizans's midfield versatility helped CSKA to win the Russian cup and finish league runners-up. He followed up with a crucial goal in the amazing Euro play-off fightback against Turkey.

GREAT MOMENTS FROM THE PAST

Penalties and golden goals make all the difference as France fulfil their promise to take the European crown and follow up their World Cup triumph... the outstanding player of the tournament, ball-playing magician Zinedine Zidane, keeps a cool head in the semi-final, then Wiltord and Trezeguet turn Italy inside out in Rotterdam as they snatch late victory from the jaws of defeat. Italy are devastated as the sweet smell of success turns very sour indeed.

Euro 2000 – the most exciting and entertaining of the modern era by the judgement of many critics – made headlines right from the start when they were awarded jointly to Holland and Belgium. The expansion of the finals in 1996 to incorporate 16 national teams had made it inevitable that event-sharing would be necessary and, in this way, UEFA set a precedent which FIFA would grudgingly follow when it awarded the 2002 World Cup to be hosted jointly by Japan and South Korea. In the event, this tournament was fit to rival any World Cup finals.

Above: Golden Goal: David Trezeguet smashes the ball past Francesco Toldo in the Italian goal to bring the European Championship to a sudden halt with France now crowned kings of European as well as world football **Right:** Toldo can't quite believe it as Sylvain Wiltord scores a late, late equaliser to kill off Italian hopes of sweet, sweet victory

This was also the second event in three to be decided on a golden goal. David Trezeguet stabbed home France's winner after 112 minutes of the final against Italy – who had been leading 1–0 until the last minute of normal time. France thus became the first country since West Germany in the 1970s to lay simultaneous claim to being both world and European champions.

The finals were also disfigured by problems with England hooligans. The main 'battleground' was Charleroi when England came up against Germany in Group A. Ironically, neither of these football heavyweights qualified for the quarter-finals, Romania and Portugal going through instead. England, under Kevin Keegan, began badly by dropping a two-goal lead and losing 3–2 to Portugal for whom Nuno Gomes scored twice. A 53rd-minute header from skipper Alan Shearer provided a 1–0 win over Germany but defensive mistakes meant a 3–2 defeat by Romania.

Germany suffered an even worse fate, finishing rock bottom of the group after a 1–1 draw with Romania, the defeat by England and an embarrassing 3–0 thrashing by Portugal for whom Sergio Conceicao scored a hat-trick.

Group B was a disappointment for co-hosts Belgium despite having won the tournament's opening match 2–1 against Sweden in Brussels. Subsequent 2–0 defeats by Italy and Turkey meant the Belgians did not reach the last eight.

Group C came up with the predicted progress of Spain and Yugoslavia with the Slavs featuring in two of the finals' most memorable matches, a 3–3 draw against debutants Slovenia – who had led 3–0 at half-time – and a 4–3 defeat by Spain.

Group D was the so-called 'group of death' featuring co-hosts and favourites Holland, world champions France, 1996 runners-up Czech Republic and 1992 winners Denmark. Ironically, winners and losers were sorted out after the first two of the three matchdays with France and Holland cruising clear.

All four quarter-finals went to form and were decided within the 90 minutes. Portugal, Italy, Holland and France all progressed according to predictions, with Patrick Kluivert hitting a hat-trick in the Dutchmen's monumental 6-1 thrashing of Yugoslavia.

The Dutch went from delirium to depression, however, in the semi-finals as they went down 3–1 on penalties to Italy after a 0–0 extra-time draw. Italy, having played all but the first 33 minutes, with only 10 men after the expulsion of Gianluca Zambrotta, emerged in triumph from one of the most momentous defensive battles in even their negative history. "It will take a great team to beat us," said Italy captain Paolo Maldini after the victory over the Dutch but France proved just that in the final in Rotterdam.

To reach the final the French had edged Portugal on a last-minute golden goal penalty by Zinedine Zidane in their semi in Brussels. Portugal had led through Nuno Gomes after 18 minutes and it was not until after the interval that Arsenal's Thierry Henry equalised. That goal sent the duel into extra-time and it was decided only seconds short of the full 120 minutes after referee Gunther Benko ruled controversially that Abel Xavier had handled. Furious Portuguese protests held up

the match for several minutes before Zidane stroked home the decisive spotkick cool as you like.

France left it late again in the final against Italy in Rotterdam. Italy traded raid for raid in a goalless first half and took the lead 11 minutes after the interval through Marco Delvecchio. Even man of the tournament Zidane couldn't work his usual magic as the match ran into stoppage time with the Italians still clinging to their advantage.

Then, seconds from the whistle, Sylvain Wiltord punished fatigue in the *Azzurri* defence with a late, late equaliser. Italy, now worse off both psychologically and physically, subsided 13 minutes into extra-time when David Trezeguet found crucial space and time for his golden goal. That opportunism, ironically, earned Trezeguet a transfer to Italy's Juventus.

ICONS OF PORTUGUESE FOOTBALL

The Portuguese are known as "the Brazilians of Europe" because of the exhuberance with which they traditionally express themselves out on the pitch. For sheer technique, silky passing skills and ability to reproduce the Beautiful Game, few nations can match them. In terms of trophies, the national side may be underachievers, but the roll call of great players the country has given to the world is amazing, and here we feature the crème de la crème.

MARIO COLUNA

Mario Coluna was commander of the Portuguese national team which reached the World Cup semi-finals in 1966 and midfield general of Benfica's outstanding club side of the 1960s.

Born in Mozambique, Coluna was an outstanding all-round sportsman as a teenager. His local long-jump record stood for years beyond the summer of 1954 when he was lured away to Lisbon by Benfica. Originally a centre-forward, there was no immediate opportunity for Coluna because of the dominance in that role of Benfica's top-scoring captain, Jose Aguas.

But when Aguas was injured Coluna grabbed his chance with both feet. When Aguas regained fitness, the Brazilian coach Otto Bumbel used them as a twin strike force and even occasionally played Coluna on the wing. He was converted into his most successful role, as an inside-left, however, by Bela Guttman, Bumbel's successor.

Guttman, an exiled Hungarian, still believed in the old WM system and saw in Coluna an old-fashioned inside forward. He could run and work, read the game and score goals – he was the fulcrum of Benfica's attack when they won the European Champions Cup for the first time in 1961.

Benfica's path had been eased by the first-round defeat of holders Real Madrid by Barcelona. In the final in Bern, Barcelona were clear favourites to beat Benfica but they had reckoned without Coluna. Benfica were 2–1 up early in the second half, but under heavy pressure when they broke forward and Coluna smacked a half-volley past Barcelona keeper Antonio Ramallets from 30 yards. It proved just enough as Benfica went on to clinch a 3–2 win and their first European crown.

Above: Portugal's Mario Coluna and Dominic Cavem run off a few pounds in preparation for their World Cup qualifier against England in 1962 **Right:** Bobby Charlton and Coluna exchange pennants before the European Cup final at Wembley in 1968. Manchester United beat Benfica 4–1

Pulling the strings

That summer, Guttman began to recast his team. The club had discovered a wonderful young striker named Eusebio whom Guttman saw as an eventual successor to Aguas as the team's top marksman. But while a new strike force settled down, Coluna's ability to pull the midfield strings grew more important. Thus Benfica won a second European Cup, this time beating Real Madrid 5–3 in a thriller in Amsterdam, with Coluna again contributing a remarkable long-range goal.

Guttman retired after the final and was replaced by the Chilean, Fernando Riera. Riera was a devotee of 4-2-4 and immediately switched Coluna into the vital role on the left of midfield. Benfica duly cruised through to a third successive Champions Cup Final, against Milan at Wembley. They appeared on their way to victory too after Eusebio fired them ahead. But Milan had other, ruthless ideas.

They had identified Coluna as the danger man, more influential overall than Eusebio, and picked midfielder Gino Pivatelli specifically to mark him. With half an hour gone, Pivatelli did just that – landing, two-footed on Coluna's left ankle. Substitutes not being permitted then, Coluna hobbled through the rest of the game and Benfica lost 2–1.

Three years later, Coluna was back at Wembley for the peak of his career in the 1966 World Cup.

Coluna had been born in Mozambique but, since it was then a Portuguese colony, he qualified to play for the country of his adoption. He made his debut in 1955 and was established as playmaker and skipper by the time the 1966 World Cup finals came around.

In England, the Portuguese were appearing in the finals for the first time. Brazilian Otto Gloria was coach, Coluna was anchor man and Eusebio was the attacking hammer. As so often happened, Eusebio grabbed most of the headlines, but the connoisseurs kept their eyes on Coluna. Portugal finished third, their best-ever World Cup ranking, after beating the Soviet Union 2–1 at Wembley.

Three years after the defeat by Milan, Coluna had returned to the Empire stadium in glory. Gloria said: "Coluna is one of the players I have most admired in my career. Football is a team game. You can have all the outstanding individuals you like, but if you have no one to organise the team itself then the individual talent is wasted. That's what Coluna did for me in 1966: he pulled all the strings and, most important, all the other players respected him not only as a footballer but as a man."

By now 31, and with 73 caps to his credit, he decided to wind down his career and return to Mozambique where, after independence in the mid-1970s, he served as first national coach and later as Minister for Sport. That was Mario Coluna: always the man to run the show.

Mario Esteves Coluna

1935: Born on August 6 in Laurenço Marques, Mozambique

1954: Played in midfield for Laurenço Marques, a nursery team for Portuguese giants, Sporting Lisbon

1955: Joined Benfica in the Portuguese capital and played with them until 1970, winning 10 league titles and numerous cups in the process. In 1970, he moved on to Lyon in France and played one more season with them

1966: Reached the semi-final of the World Cup with Portugal

1994: Became Minister of Sport in Mozambique, and later graduated to President of the Mozambique Football Association

1997: Voted on to a list of the 100 Greatest Footballers Of All Time, as chosen by *La Republica* newspaper, Italy

EUSEBIO

Think of Portuguese football and the indelible image is of Eusebio, the so-called 'Brown Bomber' or 'Black Panther,' striding through the shattered defences of the 1966 World Cup finals. He was the tournament's nine-goal top scorer at just 24 years of age.

Yet though Eusebio is considered the greatest Portuguese footballer he was born and brought up in Mozambique, then one of Portugal's African colonies. Eusebio's true claim might thus be as the first great African player to bestride the world stage.

Portuguese giants such as Benfica, Sporting and FC Porto financed nursery teams in Mozambique and neighbouring Angola and transported a wealth of talent into not only the Portuguese league but into the national team.

Eusebio was a junior product not of Benfica but of their great Lisbon rivals, Sporting. But when Sporting summoned him to Lisbon for a trial in 1961, he was kidnapped off the aeroplane by Benfica and hidden away until Sporting had lost interest.

Hungarian coach Bela Guttman was many years ahead of his time in his high regard for African players. Stars he encouraged at Benfica included long-time fan favourites such as goalkeeper Alberto da Costa Pereira, centre-forward Jose Aguas and inside forwards Joaquim Santana and Mario Coluna.

Head to head with Pele

Eusebio's turn to join the party came at the end of the 1960–61 season. Benfica had just won the European Champions Cup for the first time and their duel with Pele's Santos in the Paris Tournament was hyped as an unofficial world club championship.

It also appeared extremely one-sided since Benfica went in at half-time 3–0 down. Guttman, with nothing to lose, sent on Eusebio as a substitute. Benfica still lost but 'only' by 5–4 and Eusebio fired a spectacular hat-trick to outshine even Pele. He was off and running.

Twelve months later Eusebio rammed home two characteristic cannonball goals in Benfica's 5–3 victory over Real Madrid in the Champions Cup Final in Amsterdam. And so it went on.

In 13 seasons he helped Benfica win the league seven times and the cup twice; he was European Footballer of the Year in 1965 and top scorer with nine goals in the 1966 World Cup finals in England; he was scorer of 38 goals in 46 internationals, as well as being the league's leading scorer seven times before knee trouble forced a temporary early retirement at 32.

Wembley stadium played major roles in Eusebio's career. It was at Wembley, in a 2–0 World Cup qualifying defeat by England in 1961, that his youthful power first made

Eusebio Da Silva Ferreira

1942: Born Eusebio Da Silva Ferreira on January 25 in Laurenço Marques, Mozambique

1952: Joined the youth teams of Sporting (Laurenço Marques), a nursery team for the Portuguese giants of the same name

1961: Sporting tried to bring Eusebio to Lisbon, but he was 'kidnapped' on arrival by Benfica. In the autumn with barely a dozen league games to his name, he made his debut for Portugal

1965: Voted European Footballer of the Year

1966: Crowned top-scorer with nine goals, as Portugal finished third in the World Cup finals in England, where he was nicknamed 'the new Pele' and 'the Black Panther'

1969: Won Portuguese championship medal for the seventh and last time with Benfica before winding down his career in Mexico and Canada

1992: A statue in his honour was unveiled at the entrance to Benfica's Estadio da Luz in Lisbon

the international game sit up; two years later it was back at Wembley, in 1963, that he claimed a superb individual goal as consolation for Benfica's 2–1 Champions Cup final defeat by Milan; and it was at Wembley again that Eusebio led Portugal to their best-ever third place in the World Cup, in 1966.

Eye for goal

His exploits in those finals are written large in World Cup legend. He went goalless from the 3–1 win over Hungary but scored once in a 3–0 defeat of Bulgaria and twice in the 3–1 beating of Brazil which lifted Portugal into the quarter-finals. Here he grabbed four goals in the amazing 5–3 turnaround defeat of North Korea, after the Koreans had been leading 3–0, and then rammed home a penalty in the subsequent 2–1 defeat by England in the semis.

Back at Wembley for the third-place play-off, Eusebio opened the scoring with another spot-kick in Portugal's 2–1 win over the Soviet Union. Rapturous English fans stood to salute him at the end.

Great ambassador

Two years later, Eusebio was back again at Wembley, displaying the character which earned him recognition not only as a great player but as a great sportsman too.

In the closing minutes of yet another Champions Cup final, with Benfica and Manchester United level 1–1, Eusebio was brilliantly foiled by United keeper Alex Stepney. His generously spontaneous reaction was to pat Stepney on the back.

In the 1970s, despite the knee problem, Eusebio could not resist an appeal from ex-Benfica team-mate Antonio Simeos to make a comeback in the fledgling North American Soccer League. He played alongside Simoes for Boston Minutemen and then with Toronto Metros-Croatia and Las Vegas Quicksilver. When the NASL collapsed, he returned home to Portugal to take up various appointments as television analyst, as assistant coach and as the most honoured public face of Benfica.

Appropriately, a statue of Eusebio now stands at the entrance to Benfica's stadium.

Above: Me and my shadow: Eusebio seldom managed to get more than a few feet away from England's hardman Nobby Stiles during the World Cup semi-final at Wembley in 1966. England's plan to stifle 'the Black Panther' by whatever means necessary proved highly effective, and they ran out 2–1 winners **Left:** Eusebio before the game

VITOR BAIA

Portugal's goalkeepers down the years have been a very mixed bunch – from the extravagant Joao Azevedo in the 1940s, to the erratic Alberto Costa Pereira in the late 1950s, the unpretentious Jose Pereira (no relation) in the late 1960s, and then the towering Vitor Damas in the 1970s.

But none held the fort as long, or anything like as effectively, as Vitor Manuel Martins Baia.

The surprise twist about an international career which spanned 80 caps between 1990 and 2002 was that Baia's family were fanatical Benfica fans, and he only went for a trial with great rivals FC Porto in the first place to keep another player company.

"I really had never thought of myself making the grade as a professional," said Baia years later. "I had nothing to lose when we went for a trial, so I was completely relaxed about it. Maybe that was the reason I did well."

Baia, born on October 15, 1969, quickly rose through the Porto ranks and was thrown in at the deep end in the 1988–89 season.

The club's experienced Polish keeper, Joszef Mlynarczyk was injured while Portugal international Ze Beto was suspended. Porto had no option but to promote Baia and quickly saw their faith rewarded.

Footballer of the Year

In 1992 he was voted Portugal's Footballer of the Year, a rare honour for any goalkeeper but especially for one so young. That year he had set a domestic league record by not conceding a goal in more than 1,000 minutes and his fame soon spread well beyond the confines of the Portuguese game.

Baia's inspirational maturity between the posts made it even more of a surprise when his temper boiled over in the spring of 1996 and he was subsequently suspended after being sent off for his role in a dust-up between players and officials during a game against Campo Maiorense. A lengthy ban would have threatened Baia's presence in Portugal's goal at the European Championship in England, the seniors' first appearances in a major finals tournament for a decade.

Practical common sense won the day though, and Baia was suspended for 'only' two months. The big goalkeeper thus returned just in time to join Porto's league title-winning celebrations, and then help Portugal reach the quarter-finals at Euro 96 – where they lost narrowly to the Czech Republic.

At Porto, Baia had progressed impressively under Bobby Robson, so when the former England manager was lured away to Barcelona in the summer of 1996, he

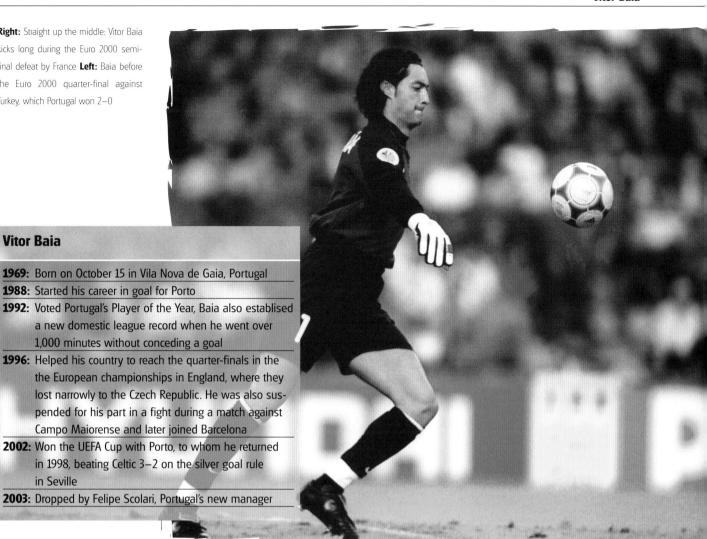

Vitor Baia

1969: Born on October 15 in Vila Nova de Gaia, Portugal

1988: Started his career in goal for Porto

1992: Voted Portugal's Player of the Year, Baia also establised a new domestic league record when he went over 1,000 minutes without conceding a goal

1996: Helped his country to reach the quarter-finals in the the European championships in England, where they lost narrowly to the Czech Republic. He was also suspended for his part in a fight during a match against Campo Maiorense and later joined Barcelona

2002: Won the UEFA Cup with Porto, to whom he returned in 1998, beating Celtic 3–2 on the silver goal rule in Seville

2003: Dropped by Felipe Scolari, Portugal's new manager

took not only assistant coach Jose Mourinho with him but also Baia, his goalkeeper.

In his initial spell with Porto, Baia won four league titles and two cups and the lucky touch was maintained throughout his first season in Spain when Barcelona won the European Cup-Winners' Cup against holders Paris Saint-Germain in Rotterdam.

But Baia's career was completely turned upside down a few weeks later when Barcelona promoted Robson 'upstairs' and brought in Dutch coach Louis Van Gaal from Ajax.

One man's meat

Van Gaal had his own ideas about goalkeepers and Baia's style was not for him. Just as Robson had brought Baia with him, so Van Gaal brought Dutchman Ruud Hesp in his wake.

Baia lasted just two matches under Van Gaal before being relegated to the subs' bench and then into the stand. Halfway through the season, he had no option but to return to Porto. Morale and confidence is crucial to any footballer but it is paramount for a goalkeeper. Baia fought back from his Barcelona humiliation, regained his form and his place in the national team for both Euro 2000 and then the 2002 World Cup.

Portugal went to Korea and Japan as one of the fancied dark horses. But over-confidence prompted a 3–2 opening defeat by the United States and they never recovered from the shock.

Baia found himself virtually abandoned in goal by a ramshackle defence and the Portuguese crashed out in the first round after a bad-tempered 1–0 defeat by the Koreans.

That bad-tempered reversal in Incheon was Baia's 79th international and he played No 80 at the start of the following season when Portugal drew 1–1 with England in a friendly at Villa Park, Birmingham. It was apparently the end of the road. Baia was substituted at half-time by Ricardo from neighbours Boavista and was not seen again all season.

Yet his international experience continued to pay dividends for club if not country. Porto became the first Portuguese club to carry off the UEFA Cup when they – and Baia – held their nerve to beat Celtic 3–2 on the silver goal rule in the final in Seville. Footballing life has not been too kind to Vitor Baia in the run-up to these championships. Despite criticism in the Portuguese press, Brazil-born national coach Felipe Scolari has refused to reinstate him in the national side, and he has even been dropped by Porto boss Jose Mourinho. Nothing, however, can detract from Baia's status as an all-time great of Portuguese football.

LUIS FIGO

For a player whose face wears such a serious expression of professional duty, it is hard to believe that Luis Figo is a specialist in controversy. But his talents have made him both one of the world's finest wingers and one of the game's most perceptive creative forces.

The tale of his earth-shattering move from Barcelona to Real Madrid in the summer of 2000 for a then world record £37million is legend. Not so well documented is the original international pursuit for Figo back in the spring of 1995.

Tug of love

He was already an established international with four goals in 23 matches for Portugal when both Parma and Juventus came calling. Both Italian clubs claimed his signature and the row went to FIFA for arbitration. The world authority ruled both agreements invalid and banned Figo from a move to Italy for two years. That suited Barcelona who jumped in at high speed to snap him up for a bargain £1.5million.

Figo never regretted the move for a moment. He was hailed as Europe's most dangerous outside-right, was appointed Barcelona captain and won various titles and trophies under the management of Dutchman Louis Van Gaal.

He said: "It's like destiny. When I decided I wanted to leave Sporting Lisbon the possibility of joining Barcelona was non-existent. But if they had been bidding from the start, then I would have signed for them with my eyes shut."

Figo had already recognised that, if he were to achieve all his ambitions, he needed a high-profile club as his stage. That was the drawback to coming from Portugal, a country which could never aspire to being a permanent member of the European elite alongside the likes of Italy, Spain, England, Germany and France.

As he once said: "A Spanish player has a much better chance of appearing at the highest level because that's a country which is almost always present at the finals tournaments of World Cups or European Championships. An individual player from outside has to fight harder to be recognized on his own merits."

But Figo was recognised as one of Europe's outstanding talents from his teenage days. He joined top Lisbon outfit Sporting Clube of Portugal at 11, was a European champion at Under-16 level in 1989 in Denmark and a World Youth Cup winner in 1991 against Brazil in Lisbon. Coach Carlos Queiroz saw Figo as a star of the so-called 'golden generation' as he proved when Portugal reached the finals of the European Under-21 Championship in France in 1994.

He had also already been marked out as leadership material and captained Sporting to victory in the Portuguese cup in his last season, in

1995, when he was still only 23. That was when the giants of Italy and Spain decided they should wait no longer and, once Parma and Juventus had confused the transfer issue, he signed for Barcelona.

Shock waves

Figo arrived in Catalonia in the latter days of the team management of Johan Cruyff but found success there under his Dutch successor, Van Gaal. That meant winning the European Cup-Winners' Cup, Spanish cup and European Supercup in 1997, the domestic league and cup double in 1998 and the Spanish league championship again in 1999.

On the international stage, Figo made his Portugal debut in 1991 and starred in the run to the quarter-finals of Euro 96 and semi-finals of Euro 2000. It was after an explosive golden goal defeat by France that Figo starred in an even more sensational transfer drama.

Millionaire property developer Florentino Perez won the Real Madrid presidential elections by promising to sign Figo – which he did for a then world record fee of £37million. But even the size of the fee was nothing compared with the shock waves which rocked not only Barcelona but all Spanish football.

It was a brave move by Figo which has cast him in the role of ultimate hate figure for the Barcelona faithful. But in career terms, it was also the right move.

Since pulling on the pristine all-white of Madrid, he has won the Champions League, the World Club Cup, the Spanish league twice and been hailed as both FIFA World Player of the Year and as European Footballer of the Year.

All that remains to be won is a major trophy at national team level...

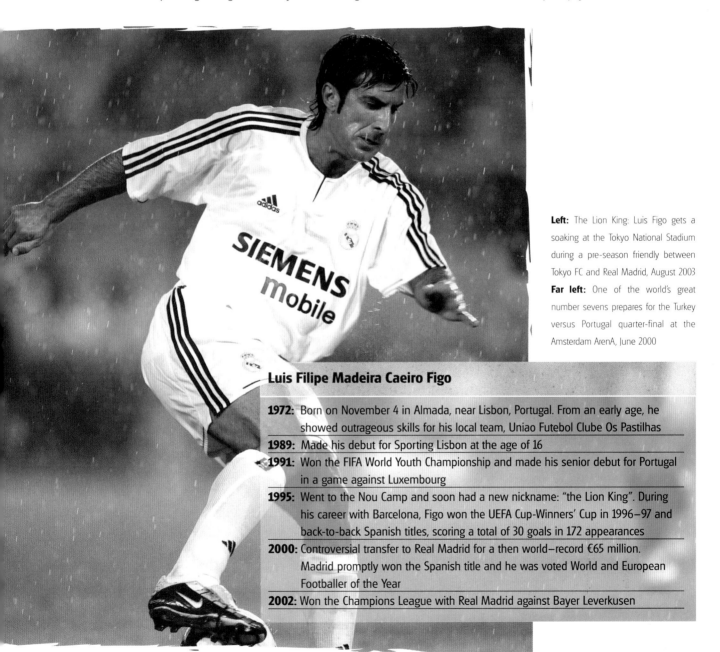

Left: The Lion King: Luis Figo gets a soaking at the Tokyo National Stadium during a pre-season friendly between Tokyo FC and Real Madrid, August 2003
Far left: One of the world's great number sevens prepares for the Turkey versus Portugal quarter-final at the Amsterdam ArenA, June 2000

Luis Filipe Madeira Caeiro Figo

1972: Born on November 4 in Almada, near Lisbon, Portugal. From an early age, he showed outrageous skills for his local team, Uniao Futebol Clube Os Pastilhas
1989: Made his debut for Sporting Lisbon at the age of 16
1991: Won the FIFA World Youth Championship and made his senior debut for Portugal in a game against Luxembourg
1995: Went to the Nou Camp and soon had a new nickname: "the Lion King". During his career with Barcelona, Figo won the UEFA Cup-Winners' Cup in 1996–97 and back-to-back Spanish titles, scoring a total of 30 goals in 172 appearances
2000: Controversial transfer to Real Madrid for a then world–record €65 million. Madrid promptly won the Spanish title and he was voted World and European Footballer of the Year
2002: Won the Champions League with Real Madrid against Bayer Leverkusen

EUROPEAN CHAMPIONSHIP CHRONOLOGY

Surprisingly the last of the great continental competitions to get under way, the European Championship has evolved, after a stuttering start, into a glamorous tournament to rival the World Cup. But there's been much skulduggery and heavy politicking along the way...

1927
▶ Henri Delaunay, of the French federation, proposes a European Championship at a meeting of the world governing body, FIFA.

1954
▶ UEFA, a specific European football federation, is founded.

1955
▶ Henri Delaunay dies but he is succeeded as general secretary of the French federation by his son, Pierre, who determines to turn his father's dream into reality.

1957
▶ UEFA proposes launching a European championship at its Copenhagen congress on June 28. The votes sees 14 federations in favour (Czechoslovakia, Denmark, East Germany, France, Greece, Hungary, Luxembourg, Poland, Portugal, Romania, Soviet Union, Spain, Turkey and Yugoslavia), and seven against (Belgium, Finland, Holland, Italy, Norway, Switzerland and West Germany), with five abstentions (England, Northern Ireland, Scotland, the Republic of Ireland and Sweden).

1958
▶ On August 6, UEFA formally launches the event with a draw for the first rounds and the decision to honour the vision of Henri Delaunay by naming the trophy in his memory. The French federation presents the trophy and is awarded hosting rights to the first finals.
▶ Some 17 federations enter, meaning one preliminary tie is necessary. Czechoslovakia and the Irish Republic are drawn to contest it.
▶ On September 28 the ball is set rolling in the Lenin Stadium in Moscow with a first-round, first-leg tie between the Soviet Union and Hungary. The Soviets win 3–1 and the first goal in the entire history of the competition is scored after four minutes by Anatoly Ilyin, an outside-left with Spartak Moscow.

1959
▶ In the single qualifying round tie, the Republic of Ireland beat the Czechoslovaks 2–0 in Dublin on April 5, but lose 4–0 away on May 10 to go out 4–2 on aggregate.

1960
▶ The event's first political crisis follows the pairing of the Soviet Union with Spain in the quarter-finals. General Francisco Franco's regime refuses to issue visas for the Soviets who thus qualify for the semi-finals on a walkover.
▶ The first final is staged in the old Parc des Princes, Paris, on July 10. The Soviet Union defeat Yugoslavia 2–1. Arthur Ellis of England is the referee.

1962
▶ An increased 29 countries enter the 1964 Nations Cup. West Germany remain absent, but England compete for the first time. More political problems see Greece refuse to play neighbours Albania who are duly awarded a walkover.
▶ On October 3 England make their competition debut against France at Hillsborough, Sheffield. England's first match under new manager Alf Ramsey ends 1–1.

1963
▶ England crash out after losing their return against France 5–2 in Paris and thus go down 6–3 on aggregate.

1964
▶ UEFA designates Spain as the venue for the second finals even before the Spanish national team qualifies. The Spanish government guarantees no political problems, whoever qualifies.
▶ Spain become the second European champions, beating the Soviet Union 2–1 in the Estadio Bernabeu in Madrid on June 21. Again the referee is English, Arthur Holland.

1966

▶ Increasing popularity means 31 of UEFA's 33 members enter the third championship. The first round is reorganised on a mini-leagues basis rather than two-leg direct elimination. West Germany, runners-up in that summer's World Cup, enter for the first time.

1967

▶ West Germany mark their European debut on April 8 by thrashing Albania 6–0 in Dortmund. Gerd Muller scores four of the goals.

▶ The first crowd trouble in the competition erupts on November 5 in Vienna's Prater stadium when a pitch invasion forces the game between Austria and Greece to be abandoned four minutes from time.

1968

▶ Spain, Yugoslavia, the Soviet Union and Italy win knock-out, two-leg quarter-final ties. The finals are awarded to Italy who scrape ultimate victory by defeating the Soviet Union on the toss of a coin in the semi-finals and Yugoslavia in the final after the only replay (penalty shoot-outs not having yet been introduced).

1970

▶ The tournament's name is formally changed from Nations Cup to European Championship.

1972

▶ In the quarter-finals, England lose a competitive international at home to foreign opposition for the first time – going down 3–1 at Wembley to West Germany on April 29.

▶ On June 18 West Germany win the final in Brussels by 3-0 against the Soviet Union. Gerd Müller scores twice in the final and is the tournament's 11-goal overall top marksman.

1974

▶ West Germany, on July 7, become the first nation to hold both the European and world crowns after winning the World Cup 2–1 against Holland in Munich.

1976

▶ UEFA decides to introduce penalty shoot-outs for the finals which are awarded to an eastern European country, Yugoslavia, for the first time.

▶ All four matches in the finals go to extra time, but only the final itself on June 20 is decided on a shoot-out when Czechoslovakia beat holders West Germany 5–3 after a 2–2 draw in Belgrade.

1978

▶ UEFA decides to expand the next finals to eight nations, split into two groups of four with the winners meeting in the final. Italy are designated hosts and seeded direct to the finals.

1980

▶ Italy become the first nation to host the finals twice. The first serious hooliganism of the finals, on June 15, sees England fans clash with riot police in Turin. The match is interrupted when tear gas drifts over the pitch before Italy eventually win 1–0. West Germany beat Belgium 2–1 in the final.

1982

▶ For the first time, the entire UEFA membership – then 33 – enters. France, as host, are seeded direct to the finals for which knock-out semi-finals are restored but the third place play-off scrapped.

1984

▶ France win their first major international prize, defeating Spain 2–0 in the final in the new Parc des Princes in Paris. Skipper Michel Platini sets a record as nine-goal top-scorer in the finals.

1986

▶ Again 33 nations enter. West Germany are seeded direct to the finals as hosts.

1987

▶ More hooligan trouble disrupts the qualifiers. Holland's 8–0 home win over Cyprus on October 28 is declared invalid by UEFA because a firework thrown from the crowd strikes Cyprus goalkeeper Andreas Charitou. Holland win the replay 4–0.

1988

▶ Favourites Holland beat the Soviet Union 2–0 in the final in Munich.

1990

▶ Sweden are confirmed as hosts and thus, automatically, reach the European finals for the first time in their history.

1991

▶ Yugoslavia, despite increasing problems in the Balkans, top their qualifying group ahead of Denmark, Northern Ireland, Austria and the Faroe Islands.

1992

▶ On May 30, just 11 days before the start of the finals, the United Nations imposes trade sanctions on war-torn Yugoslavia. UEFA immediately replaces them at the finals with group runners-up Denmark.

▶ Amazingly, Denmark win the event, defeating Germany 2–0 in the final in Gothenburg on June 26.

1994

▶ UEFA expands the finals to 16 nations and awards the event to England. The fragmentation of eastern Europe after the collapse of the Soviet Union and Yugoslavia prompts a record entry of 48 nations.

1996

▶ England open the finals with a 1–1 draw against Switzerland at Wembley on June 8. Germany win the final itself 22 days later, defeating the Czech Republic 2–1 at Wembley on a golden goal.

1998

▶ UEFA confirms its award of the 2002 finals jointly to Belgium and Holland, the first co-hosting of a major international tournament.

2000

▶ England are threatened with expulsion from the finals after their hooligan fans run riot before, during and after the group stage 1–0 defeat of Germany in Charleroi on June 17.

▶ France become the first World Cup winners to subsequently add the European crown to their current honours – beating Italy 2–1 on a golden goal in the final on July 2 in Rotterdam.

2004

▶ Portugal outmanoeuvres neighbour Spain to secure hosting rights to UEFA's top international tournament. The opportunity for revenge soon presents itself as Spain are drawn against Portugal in Group A. Other hot ties include Germany v Holland and France v England.

EUROPEAN CHAMPIONSHIP RECORDS

1960 France

Quarter-finals (two legs, home and away)

Yugoslavia bt **Portugal**	1–2,	5–1	(6–3 on agg)
France bt **Austria**	5–2,	4–2	(9–4 on agg)
Czech bt **Romania**	2–0,	3–0 (5–0 on agg)	
Russia walkover v **Spain** (withdrew)			

Semi-finals

Yugoslavia	5	(Galic 11, Zanetic 55, Knez 75, Jerkovic 77, 79)
France	4	(Vincent 12, Heutte 43, 62, Wisnieski 52)
Soviet Union	3	(V Ivanov 35, 58, Ponedelnik 64)
Czechoslovakia	0	

Third place play-off

Czechoslovakia	2	(Bubernik 58, Pavlovic 88)
France	0	

Final – July 10 – Parc des Princes, Paris

Soviet Union	2	(Metrevelli 49, Ponedelnik 113)
Yugoslavia	1	(Galic 41)

HT: 0–1. 90 min: 1–1. Att: 17,966. Ref: Ellis (Eng)

Soviet Union: Yashin, Chekheli, Maslenkin, Krutikov, Voinov, Netto, Metrevelli, V Ivanov, Ponedelnik, Bubukhin, Meshki.

Yugoslavia: Vidinic, Durkovic, Miladinovic, Jusufi, Zanetic, Perusic, Matus, Jerkovic, Galic, Sekularac, Kostic.

1964 Spain

Quarter-finals (two legs, home and away)

Denmark bt **Luxembourg**	2–2,	3–3,	1–0 (p-off, 5–5 agg)
Spain bt **Rep Ireland**	5–1,	2–0	(7–1 on agg)
Hungary bt **France**	3–1,	2–1	(5–2 on agg)
Soviet Union bt **Sweden**	1–1,	3–1	(4–2 on agg)

Semi-finals

Spain	2	(Pereda 35, Amancio 115) *after extra-time*
Hungary	1	(Bene 85)
Soviet Union	3	(Voronin 19, Ponedelnik 40, V Ivanov 88)
Denmark	0	

Third place play-off

Hungary	3	(Bene 11, Novak 107 pen, 110)
Denmark	1	(Bertelsen 81) *after extra-time*

Final – June 21 – Santiago Bernabeu, Madrid

Spain	2	(Pereda 6, Marcelino 83)
Soviet Union	1	(Khusainov 8)

HT: 1–1. Att: 125,000. Ref: Holland (Eng)

Spain: Iribar, Rivilla, Olivella, Calleja, Zoco, Fuste, Amancio, Pereda, Marcelino, Suarez, Lapetra.

Soviet Union: Yashin, Shustikov, Shesternev, Mudrik, Voronin, Anichkin, Chislenko, V Ivanov, Ponedelnik, Korneyev, Khusainov.

1968 Italy

Quarter-finals (two legs, home and away)

England bt **Spain**	1–0,	2–1	(3–1 on agg)
Italy bt **Bulgaria**	2–3,	2–0	(4–3 on agg)
Yugoslavia bt **France**	1–1,	5–1	(6–2 on agg)
Soviet Union bt **Hungary**	0–2,	3–0	(3–2 on agg)

Semi-finals

Yugoslavia	1	(Dzajic 85)
England	0	
Italy	0	*Italy won on toss of a coin after extra-time*
Soviet Union	0	

Third place play-off

England	2	(Charlton 39, Hurst 63)
Soviet Union	0	

Final – June 8 – Stadie Olimpico, Rome

Italy	1 (Domenghini 80)
Yugoslavia	1 (Dzajic 38) *after extra-time*

HT: 0–1. 90min: 1–1. Att: 85,000. Ref: Dienst (Swz)

Italy: Zoff, Castano, Burgnich, Guarneri, Facchetti, Ferrini, Juliano, Lodetti, Domenghini, Anastasi, Prati.

Yugoslavia: Pantelic, Fazlagic, Holcer, Paunovic, Damjanovic, Acimovic, Trivic, Pavlovic, Petkovic, Musemic, Dzajic.

Replay – June 10 – Stadie Olimpico, Rome

Italy	2 (Riva 12, Anastasi 31)
Yugoslavia	0

HT: 2–0. Att: 50,000. Ref: Ortiz de Mendibil (Spain)

Italy: Zoff, Salvadore, Burgnich, Guarneri, Facchetti, Rosato, De Sisti, Domenghini, Mazzola, Anastasi, Riva.

Yugoslavia: Pantelic, Fazlagic, Paunovic, Holcer, Damjanovic, Acimovic, Trivic, Pavlovic, Hosic, Musemic, Dzajic.

1972 Belgium

Quarter-finals (two legs, home and away)

West Germany bt **England**	3–1,	0–0	(3–1 on agg)
Belgium bt **Italy**	0–0,	2–1	(2–1 on agg)
Hungary bt **Romania**	1–1,	2–2,	(3–3 agg) 2–1 p-off
Soviet Union bt **Yugoslavia**	0–0,	3–0	(3–0 on agg)

Semi-finals

Soviet Union	1 (Konkov 53)
Hungary	0
West Germany	2 (G Müller 24, 72)
Belgium	1 (Polleunis 83)

Third place play-off

Belgium	2 (Lambert 24, Van Himst 28)
Hungary	1 (Ku 53 pen)

Final – June 18 – Heysel, Brussels

West Germany	3 (G Müller 27, 57, Wimmer 52)
Soviet Union	0

HT: 1–0. Att: 50,000. Ref: Marschall (Austria)

West Germany: Maier, Hottges, Beckenbauer, Schwarzenbeck, Breitner, Hoeness, Netzer, Wimmer, Heynckes, G Müller, E Kremers.

Soviet Union: Rudakov, Dzodzuashvili, Khurtsilava, Kaplichni, Istomin, Kolotov, Troshkin, Konkov (Dolmatov 46), Baidachni, Banishevski (Kozenkevich 65), Onishenko.

1976 Yugoslavia

Quarter-finals (two legs, home and away)

West Germany bt **Spain**	1–1,	2–0	(3–1 on agg)
Yugoslavia bt **Wales**	2–0,	1–1	(3–1 on agg)

Czechoslovakia bt **Soviet Union**	2–0,	2–2	(4–2 on agg)
Holland bt **Belgium**	5–0,	2–1	(7–1 on agg)

Semi-finals

Czechoslovakia	3 (Ondrus 20, Nehoda 115, F Vesely 118)
Holland	1 (Ondrus og 74) *after extra-time*
West Germany	4 (Flohe 65, D Müller 80, 114, 119)
Yugoslavia	2 (Popivoda 20, Dzajic 30) *after extra-time*

Third place play-off

Holland	3 (Geels 27, 106, W van de Kerkhof 39)
Yugoslavia	2 (Katalinski 43, Dzajic 82) *after extra-time*

Final – June 20 – Crvena Zvezda (Red Star), Belgrade

Czechoslovakia	2 (Svehlik 8, Dobias 25)
West Germany	2 (D Müller 28, Holzenbein 89)

HT: 2–1. 90 min: 2–2. Att: 33,000. Ref: Gonella (Italy)

Czechoslovakia	5–3 on pens, *after extra time*

Czechoslovakia: Viktor, Pivarnik, Ondrus, Capkovic, Gogh, Dobias, Panenka, Moder, Masny, Svehlik (Jurkemik 79), Nehoda.

West Germany: Maier, Vogts, Beckenbauer, Schwarzenbeck, Dietz, Wimmer (Flohe 46), Bonhof, Beer (Bongartz 79), Hoeness, D Müller, Holzenbein.

1980 Italy

GROUP 1

West Germany	1 (Rummenigge 55)
Czechoslovakia	0
Holland	1 (Kist 56 pen)
Greece	0
West Germany	3 (K Allofs 15, 60, 68)
Holland	2 (Rep 75 pen, van der Kerkhof 86)
Czechoslovakia	3 (Panenka 5, Vizek 25, Nehoda 63)
Greece	1 (Anastopoulos 11)
Czechoslovakia	1 (Nehoda 13)
Holland	1 (Kist 58)
West Germany	0
Greece	0

	P	W	D	L	F	A	Pts
West Germany	3	2	1	0	4	2	5
Czechoslovakia	3	1	1	1	4	3	3
Holland	3	1	1	1	4	4	3
Greece	3	0	1	2	2	4	1

GROUP 2

England	1 (Wilkins 32)
Belgium	1 (Ceulemans 38)
Italy	0
Spain	0
Belgium	2 (Gerets 17, Cools 64)
Spain	1 (Quini 35)

Italy	1	(Tardelli 78)
England	0	
England	2	(Brooking 18, Woodcock 62)
Spain	1	(Dani 48 pen)
Italy	0	
Belgium	0	

	P	W	D	L	F	A	Pts
Belgium	3	1	2	0	3	2	4
Italy	3	1	2	0	1	0	4
England	3	1	1	1	3	3	3
Spain	3	0	1	2	2	4	1

Third place play-off

Czechoslovakia	1	(Jurkemik 48) *Won 9–8 on pens, after extra-time*
Italy	1	(Graziani 74)

Final – June 22 – Stadie Olimpico, Rome

West Germany	2	(Hrubesch 10, 88)
Belgium	1	(Vandereycken 71 pen)

HT: 1–0. Att: 48,000. Ref: Rainea (Rom)

West Germany: Schumacher, Kaltz, Stielike, K Forster, Dietz, Briegel (Cullmann 55), Schuster, H Müller, Rummenigge, Hrubesch, K Allofs.

Belgium: Pfaff, Gerets, L Millecamps, Meeuws, Renquin, Cools, Vandereycken, Van Moer, Mommens, François van der Elst, Ceulemans.

1984 France

GROUP 1

France	1	(Platini 77)
Denmark	0	
Belgium	2	(Vandenbergh 27, Grun 44)
Yugoslavia	0	
France	5	(Platini 3, 74, 88, Giresse 32, Fernandez 43)
Belgium	0	
Denmark	5	(Ivkovic og 7, Berggren 16, Arnesen 68, Elkjaer 81, Lauridsen 83)
Yugoslavia	0	
France	3	(Platini 59, 61, 76)
Yugoslavia	2	(Sestic 31, Stojkovic 80)
Denmark	3	(Arnesen 40, Brylle 60, Elkjaer 83)
Belgium	2	(Ceulemans 25, Vercauteren 38)

	P	W	D	L	F	A	Pts
France	3	3	0	0	9	2	6
Denmark	3	2	0	1	8	3	4
Belgium	3	1	0	2	4	8	2
Yugoslavia	3	0	0	3	2	10	0

GROUP 2

West Germany	0	
Portugal	0	
Spain	1	(Carrasco 20)
Romania	1	(Boloni 34)

West Germany	2	(Voller 24, 65)
Romania	1	(Coras 46)
Portugal	1	(Sousa 51)
Spain	1	(Santillana 72)
Spain	1	(Maceda 89)
West Germany	0	
Portugal	1	(Nene 80)
Romania	0	

	P	W	D	L	F	A	Pts
Spain	3	1	2	0	3	2	4
Portugal	3	1	2	0	2	1	4
West Germany	3	1	1	1	2	2	3
Romania	3	0	1	2	2	4	1

Semi-finals

France	3	(Domergue 24, 114, Platini 119)
Portugal	2	(Jordao 73, 97) *after extra-time*
Spain	1	(Maceda 66) *Won 5–4 on pens, after extra-time*
Denmark	1	(Lerby 6)

Final – June 27 – Parc des Princes, Paris

France	2	(Platini 56, Bellone 90)
Spain	0	

HT: 0–0. Att: 47,368. Ref: Christov (Czechoslovakia)

France: Bats, Battiston (Amoros 72), *Le Roux, Bossis, Domergue, Fernandez, Giresse, Tigana, Platini, Lacombe (Genghini 79), Bellone.
*Le Roux sent off, 84min.

Spain: Arconada, Urquiaga, Salva (Roberto 84), Gallego, Senor, Francisco, Victor, Camacho, Julio Alberto (Sarabia 76), Santillana, Carrasco.

1988 West Germany

GROUP 1

West Germany	1	(Brehme 55)
Italy	1	(Mancini 51)
Spain	3	(Michel 5, Butragueno 52, Gordillo 67)
Denmark	2	(M Laudrup 25, Povlsen 85)
West Germany	2	(Klinsmann 9, Thon 85)
Denmark	0	
Italy	1	(Vialli 73)
Spain	0	
West Germany	2	(Voller 30, 51)
Spain	0	
Italy	2	(Altobelli 65, De Agostini 87)
Denmark	0	

	P	W	D	L	F	A	Pts
West Germany	3	2	1	0	5	1	5
Italy	3	2	1	0	4	1	5
Spain	3	1	0	2	3	5	2
Denmark	3	0	0	3	2	7	0

GROUP 2

Rep of Ireland	1	(Houghton 5)
England	0	
Soviet Union	1	(Rats 53)
Holland	0	
Holland	3	(Van Basten 23, 71, 75)
England	1	(Robson 53)
Soviet Union	1	(Protasov 75)
Rep of Ireland	1	(Whelan 38)
Soviet Union	3	(Aleinikov 3, Mikhailichenko 28, Pasulko 72)
England	1	(Adams 16)
Holland	1	(Kieft 82)
Rep of Ireland	0	

	P	W	D	L	F	A	Pts
Soviet Union	3	2	1	0	5	2	5
Holland	3	2	0	1	4	2	4
Rep of Ireland	3	1	1	1	2	2	3
England	3	0	0	3	2	7	0

Semi-finals

Holland	2	(R Koeman 73pen, Van Basten 88)
West Germany	1	(Matthäus 54 pen)
Soviet Union	2	(Litovchenko 59, Protasov 62)
Italy	0	

Final – June 25 – Olympiastadion, Munich

| Holland | 2 | (Gullit 33, Van Basten 54) |
| Soviet Union | 0 | |

HT: 1–0. Att: 72,300. Ref: Vautrot (France)

Holland: Van Breukelen, Van Aerle, R Koeman, Rijkaard, Van Tiggelen, Vanenburg, Wouters, E Koeman, Muhren, Gullit, Van Basten.

Soviet Union: Dasayev, Khidiatulin, Demianenko, Litovchenko, Aleinikov, Zavarov, Belanov, Mikhailichenko, Gotsmanov (Baltacha 69), Rats, Protasov (Pasulko 71).

1992 Sweden

GROUP A

Sweden	1	(Eriksson 26)
France	1	(Papin 59)
Denmark	0	
England	0	
France	0	
England	0	
Sweden	1	(Brolin 58)
Denmark	0	
Denmark	2	(Larsen 7, Elstrup 78)
France	1	(Papin 58)
Sweden	2	(Eriksson 51, Brolin 84)
England	1	(Platt 3)

	P	W	D	L	F	A	Pts
Sweden	3	2	1	0	4	2	5
Denmark	3	1	1	1	2	2	3
France	3	0	2	1	2	3	2
England	3	0	2	1	1	2	2

GROUP B

Holland	1	(Bergkamp 7)
Scotland	0	
Germany	1	(Hässler 90)
CIS	1	(Dobrovolski 63)
Germany	2	(Riedle 29, Effenberg 47)
Scotland	0	
Holland	0	
CIS	0	
Holland	3	(Rijkaard 3, Rob Witschge 15, Bergkamp 73)
Germany	1	(Klinsmann 53)
Scotland	3	(McStay 6, McClair 17, McAllister 83 pen)
CIS	0	

	P	W	D	L	F	A	Pts
Holland	3	2	1	0	4	1	5
Germany	3	1	1	1	4	4	3
Scotland	3	1	0	2	3	3	2
CIS	3	0	2	1	1	4	2

Semi-finals

Germany	3	(Hässler 11, Riedle 59, 88)	
Sweden	2	(Brolin 64, Andersson 89)	
Denmark	2	(H Larsen 5, 32)	*Won 5-4 on pens, after extra-time*
Holland	2	(Bergkamp 23, Rijkaard 85)	

Final – June 26 – Nya Ullevi, Gothenburg

| Denmark | 2 | (Jensen 18, Vilfort 78) |
| Germany | 0 | |

HT: 1–0. Att: 37,000. Ref: Galler (Switzerland)

Denmark: Schmeichel, Sivebaek (Christiansen 66), K Nielsen, L Olsen, Piechnik, Christofte, Vilfort, J Jensen, H Larsen, B Laudrup, Povlsen.

Germany: Illgner, Reuter, Kohler, Helmer, Brehme, Buchwald, Effenberg (Thom 80), Sammer (Doll 46), Hässler, Klinsmann, Riedle.

1996 England

GROUP A

England	1	(Shearer 23)
Switzerland	1	(Turkyilmaz 82 pen)
Holland	0	
Scotland	0	
Holland	2	(Jordi 66, Bergkamp 79)
Switzerland	0	
England	2	(Shearer 52, Gascoigne 79)
Scotland	0	

Scotland	1	(McCoist 36)					
Switzerland	0						
England	4	(Shearer 23 pen, 57, Sheringham 51, 62)					
Holland	1	(Kluivert 78)					

	P	W	D	L	F	A	Pts
England	3	2	1	0	7	2	7
Holland	3	1	1	1	3	4	4
Scotland	3	1	1	1	1	2	4
Switzerland	3	0	1	2	1	4	1

GROUP B

Spain	1	(Alfonso 74)
Bulgaria	1	(Stoichkov 65 pen)
France	1	(Dugarry 25)
Romania	0	
Bulgaria	1	(Stoichkov 3)
Romania	0	
France	1	(Djorkaeff 48)
Spain	1	(Caminero 85)
France	3	(Blanc 20, Penev og 62, Loko 90)
Bulgaria	1	(Stoichkov 68)
Spain	2	(Manjarin 11, Amor 84)
Romania	1	(Raducioiu 29)

	P	W	D	L	F	A	Pts
France	3	2	1	0	5	2	7
Spain	3	1	2	0	4	3	5
Bulgaria	3	1	1	1	3	4	4
Romania	3	0	0	3	1	4	0

GROUP C

Germany	2	(Ziege 26, Moller 32)
Czech Republic	0	
Italy	2	(Casiraghi 5, 52)
Russia	1	(Tsimbalar 20)
Czech Rep	2	(Nedved 5, Bejbl 36)
Italy	1	(Chiesa 18)
Germany	3	(Sammer 56, Klinsmann 77, 90)
Russia	0	
Italy	0	
Germany	0	
Czech Rep	3	(Suchoparek 7, Kuka 19, Smicer 89)
Russia	3	(Mostovoi 49, Tetradze 54, Beschastnikh 85)

	P	W	D	L	F	A	Pts
Germany	3	2	1	0	5	0	7
Czech Republic	3	1	1	1	5	6	4
Italy	3	1	1	1	3	3	4
Russia	3	0	1	2	4	8	1

GROUP D

Denmark	1	(B Laudrup 22)
Portugal	1	(Sa Pinto 53)
Croatia	1	(Vlaovic 85)
Turkey	0	
Portugal	1	(Fernando Couto 66)
Turkey	0	

Croatia	3	(Suker 53 pen, 89, Boban 80)
Denmark	0	
Portugal	3	(Figo 4, Joao Pinto 33, Domingos 83)
Croatia	0	
Denmark	3	(B Laudrup 50 84, A Nielsen 69)
Turkey	0	

	P	W	D	L	F	A	Pts
Portugal	3	2	1	0	5	1	7
Croatia	3	2	0	1	4	3	6
Denmark	3	1	1	1	4	4	4
Turkey	3	0	0	3	0	5	0

Quarter-finals

England	0	Won 4–2 on pens, after extra-time
Spain	0	
France	0	Won 5–4 on pens, after extra-time
Holland	0	
Germany	2	(Klinsmann 21 pen, Sammer 59)
Croatia	1	(Suker 51)
Czech Republic	1	(Poborsky 53)
Portugal	0	

Semi-finals

Czech Republic	0	Won 6–5 on pens, after extra-time
France	0	
Germany	1	(Kuntz 16) Won 6–5 on pens, after extra-time
England	1	(Shearer 3)

Final – June 30 Wembley

| Germany | 2 | (Bierhoff 73, 94) |
| Czech Republic | 1 | (Berger 58 pen) |

Germany won on golden goal in extra-time
HT: 0–0. 90 min: 1–1. Att: 76,000. Ref: Pairetto (It)

Germany: Köpke, Babbel, Sammer, Helmer, Strunz, Hässler, Eilts (Bode 46), Scholl (Bierhoff 69), Ziege, Klinsmann, Kuntz.

Czech Republic: Kouba, Hornak, Rada, Kadlec, Suchoparek, Poborsky (Smicer 88), Nedved, Bejbl, Berger, Nemec, Kuka.

2000 Belgium and Holland

GROUP A

Germany	1	(Scholl 28)
Romania	1	(Moldovan 5)
Portugal	3	(Figo 21, Joao Pinto 38, Nuno Gomes 59)
England	2	(Scholes 3, McManaman 18)
Romania	0	
Portugal	1	(Costinha 90)
England	1	(Shearer 52)
Germany	0	

England	2	(Shearer 41pen, Owen 45)					
Romania	3	(Chivu 22, Munteanu 48, Ganea 89 pen)					
Portugal	3	(Sergio Conceicao 35, 54, 70)					
Germany	0						

	P	W	D	L	F	A	Pts
Portugal	3	3	0	0	7	2	9
Romania	3	1	1	1	4	4	4
England	3	1	0	2	5	6	3
Germany	3	0	1	2	1	5	1

GROUP B

Belgium	2	(Goor 43, E Mpenza 46)
Sweden	1	(Mjallby 53)
Turkey	1	(Okan Burun 16)
Italy	2	(Conte 7, Inzaghi 70 pen)
Italy	2	(Totti 6, Fiore 65)
Belgium	0	
Sweden	0	
Turkey	0	
Turkey	2	(Hakan Sukur 45, 70)
Belgium	0	
Italy	2	(Di Biagio 39, Del Piero 88)
Sweden	1	(Larsson 76)

	P	W	D	L	F	A	Pts
Italy	3	3	0	0	6	2	9
Turkey	3	1	1	1	3	2	4
Belgium	3	1	0	2	2	5	3
Sweden	3	0	1	2	2	4	1

GROUP C

Spain	0	
Norway	1	(Iversen 20)
Yugoslavia	3	(Milosevic 67, 73, Drulovic 70)
Slovenia	3	(Zahovic 22, 57, Pavlin 52)
Slovenia	1	(Zahovic 13)
Spain	2	(Raul 4, Etxeberria 59)
Norway	0	
Yugoslavia	1	(Milosevic 7)
Yugoslavia	3	(Milosevic 31, Govedarica 51, Komljenovic 75)
Spain	4	(Alfonso 39, 90, Munitis 52, Mendieta 89 pen)
Slovenia	0	
Norway	0	

	P	W	D	L	F	A	Pts
Spain	3	2	0	1	6	5	6
Yugoslavia	3	1	1	1	7	7	4
Norway	3	1	1	1	1	1	4
Slovenia	3	0	2	1	4	5	2

GROUP D

France	3	(Blanc 17, Henry 19, Wiltord 90)
Denmark	0	
Holland	1	(F De Boer 88 pen)
Czech Rep	0	
Czech Rep	1	(Poborsky 35)
France	2	(Henry 7, Djorkaeff 59)

Denmark	0	
Holland	3	(Kluivert 11, R De Boer 20, Zenden 76)
Denmark	0	
Czech Rep	2	(Smicer 64, 67)
France	2	(Dugarry 8, Trezeguet 31)
Holland	3	(Kluivert 14, F De Boer 51, Zenden 57)

	P	W	D	L	F	A	Pts
Holland	3	3	0	0	7	2	9
France	3	2	0	1	7	4	6
Czech Rep	3	1	0	2	3	3	3
Denmark	3	0	0	3	0	8	0

Quarter-finals

Portugal	2	(Nuno Gomes 44, 56)
Turkey	0	
Italy	2	(Totti 33, Inzaghi 43)
Romania	0	
Holland	6	(Kluivert 24, 38, 54, Govedarica og 50, Overmars 76, 89)
Yugoslavia	1	(Milosevic 90)
Spain	1	(Mendieta 38 pen)
France	2	(Zidane 32, Djorkaeff 43)

Semi-finals

France	2	(Henry 52, Zidane 118 pen)
Portugal	1	(Nuno Gomes 19)

France won with a golden goal in extra-time

Italy	0	
Holland	0	

Italy won 3–1 on penalties, after extra-time

Final – Jul 2 Rotterdam

France	2	(Wiltord 90, Trezeguet 103)
Italy	1	(Delvecchio 10)

HT: 0–1. 90min: 1–1. Att: 48,000. Ref: Frisk (Den)

France on golden goal in extra time

France: Barthez, Thuram, Blanc, Desailly, Lizarazu (Pires 86), Djorkaeff (Trezeguet 76), Vieira, Deschamps, Dugarry (Wiltord 57), Zidane, Henry.

Italy: Toldo, Cannavaro, Nesta, Iuliano, Pessotto, Albertini, Di Biagio (Ambrosini 66), Fiore (Del Piero 53), Maldini, Totti, Delvecchio (Montella 86).

Group A

Match	Date	Time	Venue	Fixture			Score
1	Saturday June 12	5.00pm	Dragao, Porto	Portugal	v	Greece	1 - 2
2	Saturday June 12	7.45pm	Algarve, Faro/Loule	Spain	v	Russia	1 - 0
9	Wednesday June 16	5.00pm	Bessa, Porto	Greece	v	Spain	1 - 1
10	Wednesday June 16	7.45pm	Luz, Lisbon	Russia	v	Portugal	0 - 2
17	Sunday June 20	7.45pm	Algarve, Faro/Loule	Russia	v	Greece	2 - 1
18	Sunday June 20	7.45pm	Jose Alvalade, Lisbon	Spain	v	Portugal	0 - 1

Group A Final Table

Team	P	W	L	D	F	A	Pts	Top Scorers
1 PORTUGAL	3	2	0	1	4	2	6	
2 GREECE	3	1	1	1	4	4	4	
3 SPAIN	3	1	1	1	2	2	4	
4 RUSSIA	3	1	0	2	2	4	3	

12

Group B

Match	Date	Time	Venue	Fixture			Score
3	Sunday June 13	5.00pm	Estadio Municipal de Leiria	Switzerland	v	Croatia	0 - 0
4	Sunday June 13	7.45pm	Luz, Lisbon	France	v	England	2 - 1
11	Thursday June 17	5.00pm	Municipal, Coimbra	England	v	Switzerland	3 - 0
12	Thursday June 17	7.45pm	Estadio Municipal de Leiria	Croatia	v	France	2 - 2
19	Monday June 21	7.45pm	Luz, Lisbon	Croatia	v	England	2 - 4
20	Monday June 21	7.45pm	Municipal, Coimbra	Switzerland	v	France	1 - 2

Group B Final Table

Team	P	W	L	D	F	A	Pts	Top Scorers
1 FRANCE	3	2	1	0	6	4	7	
2 ENGLAND	3	2	0	1	8	4	6	
3 CROATIA	3	0	2	1	4	6	2	
4 SWISS	3	0	1	2	1	5	1	

19

Group C

Match	Date	Time	Venue	Fixture			Score
5	Monday June 14	5.00pm	Afonso Henriques, Guimaraes	Denmark	v	Italy	0 - 0
6	Monday June 14	7.45pm	Jose Alvalade, Lisbon	Sweden	v	Bulgaria	5 - 0
13	Friday June 18	5.00pm	Municipal, Braga	Bulgaria	v	Denmark	0 - 2
14	Friday June 18	7.45pm	Dragao, Porto	Italy	v	Sweden	1 - 1
21	Tuesday June 22	7.45pm	Bessa, Porto	Denmark	v	Sweden	2 - 2
22	Tuesday June 22	7.45pm	Afonso Henriques, Guimaraes	Italy	v	Bulgaria	2 - 1

Group C Final Table

Team	P	W	L	D	F	A	Pts	Top Scorers
1 SWEDEN	3	1	2	0	8	3	5	
2 DENMARK	3	1	2	0	4	2	5	
3 ITALY	3	1	2	0	3	2	5	
4 BULGARIA	3	0	0	3	1	9	0	

16

Group D

Match	Date	Time	Venue	Fixture			Score
7	Tuesday June 15	5.00pm	Municipal, Aveiro	Czech Rep.	v	Latvia	2 - 1
8	Tuesday June 15	7.45pm	Dragao, Porto	Germany	v	Holland	1 - 1
15 Saturday June 19		5.00pm	Bessa, Porto	Latvia	v	Germany	0 - 0
16	Saturday June 19	7.45pm	Municipal, Aveiro	Holland	v	Czech Rep.	2 - 3
23	Wednesday June 23	7.45pm	Jose Alvalade, Lisbon	Germany	v	Czech Rep.	1 - 2
24	Wednesday June 23	7.45pm	Municipal, Braga	Holland	v	Latvia	3 - 0

Group D Final Table

Team	P	W	L	D	F	A	Pts	Top Scorers
1 CZECH REP	3	3	0	0	7	4	9	
2 HOLLAND	3	1	1	1	6	4	4	
3 GERMANY	3	0	2	1	2	3	2	
4 LATVIA	3	0	1	2	1	5	1	

16   (64)

Quarter-Finals

Match	Date	Time	Venue	Fixture			Score
25 (QF1)	Thursday June 24	7.45pm	Luz, Lisbon	Winner A	-	Second B	
				PORTUGAL	v	ENGLAND	2 - 2 1-1 6-5
26 (QF2)	Friday June 25	7.45pm	Jose Alvalade, Lisbon	Winner B	-	Second A	
				FRANCE	v	GREECE	0 - 1
27 (QF3)	Saturday June 26	7.45pm	Algarve, Faro/Loule	Winner C	-	Second D	
				SWEDEN	v	HOLLAND	0 - 0 6-5
28 (QF4)	Sunday June 27	7.45pm	Dragao, Porto	Winner D	-	Second C	
				CZECH REP	v	DENMARK	3 - 0

8 (72)

Semi-Finals

Match	Date	Time	Venue	Fixture			Score
29	Wednesday June 30	7.45pm	Jose Alvalade, Lisbon	Winner QF1	-	Winner QF3	
				PORTUGAL	v	HOLLAND	2 - 1
30	Thursday July 1	7.45pm	Dragao, Porto	Winner QF2	-	Winner QF4	
				GREECE	v	CZECH REP	1 - 0 aet

4 (80)

Final

Match 31: Sunday July 4, 7.45pm – Luz, Lisbon

0 PORTUGAL   v   GREECE   1

Scorers

(81)

PICTURE ACKNOWLEDGEMENTS

The publishers would like to thank the following sources for their kind permission to reproduce the pictures in this book:

ACTION IMAGES 43, 50, 53, 69/Andrew Budd 47, 60/Andy Cauldridge 27, 45/ Rudy Lhomme 36, 37/ Brandon Malone 17, 21, 59/ Tony Marshall 68/ Michael Regan 52/Alex Morton 42, 44/ Darren Walsh 2-3, 39.

EMPICS/Barrats 62/Adam Davy 1, 9, 11tl, 11bl, 11br, 13ml, 13bl, 13tr, 24, 25, 34, 35, /Mark Earthy 46/Mike Egerton 6-7, 67/Nigel French 26,/Imapress 12bl, 12br,/Eric Lafargue 51/Tony Marshall 23,49, 54, 56, 57, 66 /Neal Simpson 28, 32, 33/Press Sport 30/Studio Buzzi 22/Topham Picturepoint 19/Witters 31.

GETTY IMAGES 4-5/AFP 40/Ben Bradford 48/Clive Bruskill 55, 80/Stuart Franklin 15, 58.

HULTON ARCHIVE 63.

OFFSIDE/L'EQUIPE 18.

PA PHOTOS 64.

SPORTING PICTURE (UK) LTD/Peter Bennett 61/Robin Hume 38/Nick Kidd 41/Jose Jogo Sa 12tl, 12tr.

TOPHAM PICTURE POINT 65.

Every effort has been made to acknowledge correctly and contact the source and/or copyright holder of each picture, and Carlton Books Limited apologises for any unintentional errors or omissions which will be corrected in future editions of this book.